Legal Almanac Series No. 6

THE LAW OF GUARDIANSHIPS

by RICHARD V. MACKAY
Member of the New York Bar

*This legal almanac has been revised
by the Oceana Editorial Staff*

Irving J. Sloan
General Editor

THIRD EDITION

1980 Oceana Publications, Inc.
Dobbs Ferry, New York 10522

Man individually and as a race is possible on earth only because, not for weeks or months but for years, love and the guardianship of the strong over the weak has existed. Oliverr Schreiner, *Man to Man*, Ch. 7.

Library of Congress Cataloging in Publication Data

Mackay, Richard Vance, 1909-
    Law of guardianships.

    (Legal almanac series; no. 6)
    "Revised by the Oceana editorial staff."
    Second ed. published in 1957 under title: Guardianship and the protection of infants.
    Includes index.
    1. Guardian and ward--United States. I. Sloan, Irving J. II. Oceana Publications, Inc. III. Title.
KF53.Z9M3   1980   346.7301'8   79-28375
ISBN 0-379-11128-4

TABLE OF CONTENTS

FOREWORD

The basis for the appointment of a guardian is the weakness, imcompetence, youthfulness, or other legally recognized disability under which the ward (the "ward" being the person whose disability requires the need for a guardian) labors. The duties and responsibilities of guardians of these persons, both the very young and the very old whose incapacities set them at a disadvantage in society and therefore make them vulnerable for exploitation make up the subject matter of this almanac. The law seeks to protect such wards against their weaknesses by appointing a competent person to look after them and their property. The text also examines the law relating to incompetent veterans and beneficiaries of veterans who because of non-age or incompetence are considered unable to handle their own affairs. In this connection, a discussion of the Uniform Incompetent Veterans Act which is in force in many jurisdictions in included.

A major new feature in this volume, and one that is too infrequently included in the treatment of the subject of guardianship with but the most limited discussion, is the consideration of the needs of the aged in this area. Indeed, by way of demonstrating our belief that this is a compelling subject, we begin with this very topic.

Status of Ward

Preliminary to any appointment, there must be proof of status. Status, as the word implies, is the standing of an individual in the society of which he is a member. It is a legal concept of the individual's position, and, for most purposes, must be determined by law, and, more specifically, by the laws of the jurisdiction of which the ward is a resident. That determination is, in most instances, binding upon all other states and for all other purposes. There are exceptions to this basic rule but they are called into play only under special circumstances. Status may be determined in several ways, depending upon the nature of the disability. Proof of age is fairly simple today. Insanity or other weaknesses, is generally proved by an *inquisition*, which means an examination into the sanity or insanity of other frailty of the individual. Medical evidence must be produced to show that person to be incompetent. An impartial judge hears the evidence and determines the question.

Jurisdiction

The status of the individual must be proved in the courts having *jurisdiction*. In other words, application must be made to the courts having the authority to make such an adjudication, and consequently, the appointment of the guardian. This authority must exist because the infant or incompetent person resides in or is domiciled in, or owns property located in the jurisdiction or simply because he is physically, though perhaps only temporarily, within the jurisdiction. The courts are vigilant in the protection of the rights of those suffering disabilities and where there is a doubt, as to whether there should or should not be a guardian, the courts will determine it to the best interests of the person involved.

The Guardian

Given *status* and *jurisdiction* (or to paraphrase, if the individual is determined to be a child or other incompetent person and the authority of court to act is established), the court then seeks a competent, disinterested person to act on his behalf. Preference is given to parents in the case of children or at least close relatives, and in the case of other incompetents kinship is also a strong consideration. But in either situation, the best interests of the child or other incompetent control the selection of such a person.

A legally appointed guardian has the duty to make an inventory of the property of his ward, to account for such property and increment or depreciation of such property periodically and to "settle" the account when the disability is removed. He has many other particular duties and responsibilities towards his ward which will be discussed in greater detail in this almanac. Indeed, some of the matters mentioned here already will be repeated in further detail in subsequent chapters.

Naturally, a guardian failing in these duties may be removed from office and may be held personally liable for any loss to his ward. The guardian is an officer of the court and is subject to its discipline. The guardian is not expected to perform these services without compensation and the laws of the various states make the provisions for his fees and disbursements.

The guardian's duties and responsibilities and rights over his ward cease when the disability is removed or terminated. Thus, when a child reaches his majority, when an older person for whatever reason resumes his ability to maintain himself, or an insane person is declared to be competent again, the guardianship terminates. The guardian ceases to have any official status when he himself becomes incompetent, or dies, or violates the trust placed in him by his appointment. At that point, the guardian, or someone acting in his behalf, must submit his account to the court which appointed him. If the court is satisfied that he performed his functions properly, the guardian and the surety which supplied the bond for his faithful performance, are released from any liability. If the court feels the guardian did not perform his duties faithfully, he may be surcharged (i.e., forced to reimburse the ward). The bonding company may be required to make this payment, in his default. Furthermore, his obligations will continue, since the court will not judicially settle his accounts until he has performed the conditions specified by it.

Note

In the initial planning of this volume material in the last edition (1957) of the Legal Almanac volume, *The Law of Support*, was to appear here. But in view of the fact that the topics in the latter have been up-dated and strengthened in a number of recently revised editions in the Series. Thus, the Almanac volumes, *Law of Separation and Divorce, Law of Adoption*, and *Investment Planning*, among others, contain strong chapters dealing with the issues of support and we accordingly suggest that you turn to these titles for information on the topic of support.

Chapter I

GUARDIANSHIP AND THE OLDER PERSON

Most, if not all treaties dealing with the subject of guardianship and ward, including the earlier editions of the Almanac volume on this topic, begin and indeed emphasize the infant ward. Indeed, the very title of the previous edition of this work was *Guardianship and the Protection of Infants*. As the original volume put it in its Introduction, "The main purpose of this almanac is to study the relationdhip of a child (i.e., the ward)to legally recognized custodian (the guardian). "

While the thrust and the bulk of the subject area even here remains the infant-ward, still we start this present volume with the older adult both for the reasons that we wish to acknowledge the growing importance of this figure in American society and because older persons are increasingly in need of protective services of which legal guardianship is but only one most appropiately treated in a legal work of this kind.

Many adults now survive through the upper age bracket. As individuals advance from one decade to the next, capacity, either physical or mental or both, tend to diminish. And more and more of these older people have some assets, be they only old age assistance. The assets are useless unless converted into goods and services that can be utilized by their owner. Better techniques both for finding those in need of help and for psycho-social-medical diagnoses have made it possible to identify more of the *incompetent* aging and at earlier stages. In the meantime, laws have been modified and the definition of the individuals for whom, a guardian may be appointed has been broadened. It is no longer restricted to those legally "insane."

Furthermore, those in the oldest age brackets are less likely to have family members or friends who might give enough informal help to avoid the necessity for legal procedures. Their natural protectors may have died, moved away or themselves reached an age where they cannot carry this kind of responsibility. Today one often finds both parent and child in older age brackets and both in need of assistance in managing their assets.

Increased mobility of the population has added to the problem in using guardianship proceedings. Many older persons travel extensively. Some spend part of the year in one state and part in another. Inability to manage for themselves may overtake them while away from their legal domiciles. The need for immediate care may arise in one jurisdiction while the assets may be in another. Or, if

1

these transients have assets with them, the legal right to appoint a guardian outside the state of their residence may be in question. Not infrequently an older individual may have two guardians, one in the jurisdiction of residence, another where he is for the moment. In such cases the two guardians, or the two courts which supervise them, may be at odds about plans for the care of the individual and about the ways in which his assets should be used or conserved.

Three major shifts have taken place concerning the assets to be administered by older persons. (1) Although ownership of real estate now plays a less important part in our economic life, it is significant that approximatelu two-thirds of those 65 or over own their homes. (2) An increasingly important role in the economy is played by income from annuities or pensions, social security benefits and public assistance payments as distingushed from increment from capital assets. (3) The distribution of wealth has shifted, so that more people have assets which need to be administered if they become imcompetent. At the same time, however, the assets are often insufficient to pay for the labor involved in administering them, particularly through court proceedings.

These changes also affect the availability of persons to act as guardians. Relatives or close friends may have died or become unable to assume the responsibility. Since many of those who may need a guardian do not have assets beyond their living requirements, they cannot pay the costs of guardianship services. Furthermore, persons who might normally act as guardians may not have sufficient knowledge or experience to carry out the duties. These "natural" guardians may not have sufficient assets of their own to guarantee faithful performance.

Attempts have been made to adapt the probate law and its administration to the social changes which have taken place in recent years. One of the most important changes has been in the destination of the group for whom a fiduciary may be appointed. Many states have enlarged the definition to include pyschotics among those needing assistance in financial management. In some states the enlarged definition has been incorporated in the basic guardianship statute. In other states, a separate but similar procedure has been set up for those who have been so diagnosed. In such instances, different terminology is used. In some states, not all of the consequences which flow from a traditional guardianship follow from the appointment of a fiduciary under the newer procedures.

Appointment of a Conservator

The California statute establishing the institution of conservatorship as distinguished from guardianship should be noted. It is designed to reach those older persons requiring assistance in financial management as well as those who need planning for personal care and supervison. The law defines the group as "Any adult person who by reason of advanced age, illness, injury, mental weakness, intemperance, addiction to drugs or other disability, or other cause is unable to properly care for himself or for his property, or who for said causes or any other cause is likely to be deceived or imposed upon by artful or designing persons, or for whom a guardian could be appointed (under Division 4 of the code) or who voluntarily requests the same and to the satisfaction the court establishes good cause therefore."

In appointing a conservator, the court is guided by what appears to be the best interest of the person placed under the conservatorship. The California law provides for flexibility in the extent to which a conservator shall take over financial management and in extending or limiting the authority as circumstances change. Provision is also made for the appointment of a temporary conservator to act in emergencies.

It should be pointed out, however, that the law governing conservatorships is substantially similar to that governing guardianship. That is, conservatorship proceedings are no less formal or expensive than guardianship proceedings. Flexibility remains limited.

Appointment of a "Legal Representative" for Public Assistance Recipients

Another recent adaptation of traditional guardianship has developed in response to the special needs of incompetents entitled to public assistance. In order to protect the rights of individuals receiving or entitled to public assistance, the Bureau of Family Services of the Department of Health, Education, and Welfare requires the appointment of a legal guardian for any recipient unable to manage his own affairs. This requirement further protected beneficiaries from pressure by the assistance-giving agency with respect to how they expend the benefits. Under this provision, federal funds could not be allocated to the states for any public assistance grant not paid directly to the recipient or a court-appointed guardian. Because of the many difficulties encountered in working within such a legal structure, a simpler procedure has been devised. An amendment to the Social Security Act now provides that federal funds may be used for matching state funds if the grant is paid to a legal representative appointed for an incompetent recipient. Several states have enacted such laws.

The essential difference between a legal representative and a legal guardian is that the former is responsible neither for the person of the incompetent nor for assets other than the public assistance grant. This fact makes it easier to find persons willing to assume the responsbility. This fact makes it easier to find person willing to assume the fiduciary responsbility. It has the disadvantage of leading the individual without the protection of someone reponsible for him as a person and for his other assers. While these are necessarily minimal in value they may be very important to him. Under the

Under the personal representative provisions certain designated public employees are empowered to sign a petition for the appointment of a legal representative. Although in about half the states "any persons," including a public employee, may sign such a petition, social workers have hesitated to assume this burden as individuals rather than in an official capacity.

Administrative Procedures

A. Accounting Procedures

Some probate courts have developed a ticker system to remind the court when a current accounting is due. Without such a system, an estate might go on idefinitely without an accounting, with no awareness of the fact by the judge.

B. Reducing Expenses for Small Estates

Some probate courts provide for waiver of court costs in estates that do not exceed a certain total value. Arrangements of this sort are frequently made on behalf of veterans and their dependents, either by state law or by court rule. A more detailed discussion of veteran's guardianships is presented in chapter 5.

Attempts have been made to meet the urgency of the need for an attorney and for a fiduciary where there is no one close to an incompetent to perform this function. In several cities, legal aid societies furnish free service to small estates. In some countries, the state's attorneys will do the necessary legal work, especially in cases where the estate includes public assistance. In many instances attorneys on boards of private social agencies do yeoman service . The Veterans Administration also provides free legal services in small estates consisting wholly, or primarily, of veteran's benefits.

C. Provisions of a Fiduciary Service

The need for someone to act as fiduciary is met in different ways. One device is appointed in each county of an official, known as the public guardian. In some states, notably Illinois, this is a fee office; that is, the public guardian does not receive a salary but depends upon fees collected from the estates he handles. This does not solve the problem of providing service for those who need their total assets for support. It does, however, make it possible to find a fiduciary for incompetents without relatives or friends to act, if their assets are sufficient to pay for the service.

In other states, such as California, the services of the public-salaried guardians are free of charge to the imcompetent. The service is limited, however, to those who are patients in certain public institutions or who are recipients of public assistance. California also has an effective guardianship service for patients in or on the rolls of state mental hospitals. This service too is free to incompetents whose assets are limited; usual guardianship fees are collected if the estates are large enough to warrent this action. California also provides for a fiduciary without court appointment for mental hospital patients when circumstances do not require court proceedings.

Fiduciaries Without Legal Guardian Appointment For Older Persons

When the total assets of the older person are minimal or when the chief purpose is to collect and disburse a small periodic income, calling into play the full gamut of probate proceedings seems inappropriate. For this reason various ways have been devised to allow someone to act as fiduciary for an incompetent without appointment as guardian.

One such device is the Small Estates Affidavit statute. Under such a law, if the total assets of an incompetent do not exceed a certain amount, the spouse or other person designated by law may make an affidavit describing the essential facts. On the basis of the facts he is authorized to collect assets belonging to the incompetent. Even the title to an automobile may be transferred.

Similarly, many states have statutes which allow a public official or the superintendent of a state mental hospital to collect and disburse assets belonging to patients up to a given amount

Insurance companies often incorporate in policies a Facility of Payment clause. Under this clause the company may pay the insurance benefits to someone other than the insured incompetent.

These devices are useful. They avoid delay and expense, and allow for maximum flexibility. They do not, however, provide controls. If the person who has taken over the assets of an incompetent does not use them for the latter's benefit, the only recourse is to bring suit. Such a remedy is hardly practical.

Administrative Fiduciary Relationships

Under federal law, an administrative agency which provides

benefits for its clients may pay a fiduciary who is not under court control. This procedure is used by the Railroad Retirement Board and the Veterans Administration.

It is used most extensively, however, by the Bureau of Old-Age, Survivors, and Disability Insurance. The Bureau's procedure will serve as the prototype of a fiduciaryship structured through an administrative agency rather than through the courts.

Section 205 (j) of the Social Security Act provides that when the interest of an entitled individual is served thereby, and regardless of his legal competency or incompetency, The Secretary of Health, Education and Welfare may either make direct payment to the beneficiary or certify the payment for his "use and benefit to a relative or some other person."

Adult beneficiaries are paid directly unless there is convincing evidence that they are incapable of managing their benefits funds or of protecting their own interests because of a disabling mental or physical impairment.Beneficiaries under 18 years of age are ordinarily not paid directly.

The "relative" or "other person" who is selected to represent the beneficiary is called a representative payee. The authority to designate a representative payee on behalf of a beneficiary has been delegated to the Bureau of Old-Age, Survivors, and Disability Insurance by the Secretary of Health, Education, and Welfare

Only three conditions are generally considered satisfactory proofs that an adult beneficiary requires a representative payee to receive and disburse Old-Age, Survivors, and Disability Insurace benefits. These are: a court finding of incompetency, appointment of a fiduciary under state law, or medical evidence of the beneficiary's incapacity to manage benefit funds or protect his own interest.

The impairment which justifies designation of a representative payee to receive a beneficiary's check need not, however, be so severe as to warrent a judicial finding of incompetency, commitment to a mental hospital or appointment of a fiduciary under state law. The decision that a representative payee is needed relates solely to his benefits fund. It does not affect other resources the beneficiary may have, and it does not affect his civil rights.

In selecting a representative payee, the Bureau gives a preference to a spouse or other relative who has custody of the beneficiary or who demonstrates a strong and responsible interest in his personal welfare. Non-profit public or private institutions are usually selected as payees only when no relative or legal guardian meets the requisite qualifications. Although the decision that a beneficiary is incapable

6

of managing his benefits and needs a representative payee is reviewable at several levels within the administrative organization, and it is not subject to formal appeal. The Bureau, however, has an appeals procedure for review of its determination as to entitlement and other matters. Courts are the final recourse under the federal law which provides for judicial review of administrative decisions.

In many respects the duties and responsibilies of the representative payee toward the beneficiary are similar to those of a court-appointed fiduciary and include a concern for the personal welfare of the client.

Under applicable regulations (20 CFR, Subpart Q, Section 404, 1609), a representative payee is required to submit annually a written report accounting for the use and disposition of the benefits certified to him. Currently, natural or adoptive parents having physical custody of a minor or a person disabled since childhood are excused from the periodic accounting. A husband or wife payee with whom an incapable adult beneficiary is living is also excused. If the representative payee is court-appointed fiduciary required to render an annual accounting to the court, he may submit a true copy of such accounts in lieu of the form prescribed by the a Social Security Administration.

Willful conversion to benefit payments received by a payee constitutes a misdemeanor punishable under law. Other appropriate remedies, including civil suit, for the recovery of misused funds are also available.

The use of benefits in the hands of a representative payee is covered by the statutes. Since Old-Age, Suvivors, and DisabilityInsurance benefits are intended to replace current income lost because of the disability, retirement or death of the insured individual, benefits are usually used for current ,maintenace. Benefit payments not needed for such maintenance must be conserved or invested. If current maintenance needs of beneficiary are being reasonably met, a portion of the benefit funds may be use to support his dependent spouse or children.

Where a beneficiary is confined in an institution because of mental or physical incapacity, the representative payee must give highest priority to the expenditure of the benefits funds for current maintenance needs, including the institution's customary charges.

In order to insure a continiuing income for current maintenance, Section 207 of the Social Security Act exempts Old-Age Survivors, or Disability Insurance benefits from execution, levy, attachment, garnishment or other seizure.

Guardianship Proceedings for Older Persons

For the most part, the description of a guardianship proceeding which will be presented in this section is close to whatever we will say subsequently in one of the chapters dealing with the infant-ward. Nevertheless, it seems useful to detail this proceeding here where we are focusing on the older person as the ward.

1. Filing the Petition

Some person, usually a close family member, who is concerned about the situation consults a lawyer. He prepares a petition outlining the facts as presented to him, including the proposed guardian it names. The petition is signed and sworn to by the person who consulted the attorney. The original petition is filed with the clerk of the court and the case is given an identifying number which is used on all pertinent documents. The clerk then sets the time and date for the hearing.

A copy of the petition together with a summons or written notice is served on the person alleged to be incompetent. In this way, he is advised of the petition, what the allegations are and when the case would be heard. These documents are handed to the alleged incompetent personally, usually by the sheriff of the country or a deputy.

2. The Court Hearing

The case is heard by the judge in the public court room at the stated time and place. The alleged incompetent is required to be present so that the judge can be satisfied by personal observation about his condition. This further assures the person in question could contest the allegations of the petition if he so desires. The judge hears relevant oral testimony from the petitioner and others usually including the alleged incompetent's doctor. If the alleged incompetent wishes to contest the case, he can testify for himself and call other witnesses. He can contest either the need for or the selection of a guardian.

3. The Determination

Following the hearing, the judge determines whether the person is in fact incompetent and, if so, who the guardian should be, and sets the amount of the fiduciary bond the guardian must then file in court. The determination is incorporated into a written order signed by the judge.

After the written order has been entered and the guardian has filed the required bond and an oath of office in which he swears to perform his duties faithfully, the clerk of the court issues what is known as Letters of Guardianship. The original document is filed in court, and one or more certified copies are delivered to the guardian. The letters are proof of the guardian's authority to act on behalf of the incompetent. He exhibits his certified copy to persons with whom he dealt in relation to the incompetent's assets.

4.Procedures of the Guardian in Managing Assets

The guardian's first job is to determine what the incompetent's assets are, to take physical possession of them, and to file a formal notice with the proper persons to show that further transactions in regard to the assets must be conducted with the guardian. This also involves filing applications for any benefits to which the incompetent might be entitled.

Once the assets are determined, the guardian lists them, showing their exact cash value, in a document called an inventory, which he signs and swears to. The inventory is then presented to the judge for his examination. On the basis of the value of the assets, the judge decides whether the original amount of the fiduciary bond is proper. If not, he enters an order cancelling the original bond and requiring a new one for the appropriate amount. From then until the case is closed, the guardian is responsibe for accounting for each item listed in the inventory.

The fiduciary bond is a document signed by the guardian guaranteeing that his maximum liability up to the amount of the bond would be paid out of pocket for losses resulting from his failure to perform his duties faithfully. The bond is also signed by two or more persons who own real estate in the country, guaranteeing that they would pay out of their own resources up to the amount of the bond if required and should the guardian fail to do so. The guardian is liable even beyond the amount of the bond, but the liability of the bondsmen is limited to the amount of their bond.

As an additional protection, the court appoints one or more appraisers, experienced in knowing the money value of different kinds of assets, to appraise the items listed in the inventory. They, like the guardian, file an oath to perform their duties properly. They report the results of their evaluation in a document called the appraisal which they sign and swear to. In this way the interests of the incompetent person are protected against mistakes in judgment (or willfully-given misinformation) on the part of the guardian. '

The estate is now a "going concern" and follows a more or less set pattern until closed. The guardian manages, invests, conserves and expends the assets of the incompetent in the manner of a prudent man managing his own affairs but with the added responsibility for doing so according to certain restriction in the law. He cannot take risks which he might normally assume in his own behalf.

In order that the court can exercise its supervision over the guardian's management, the latter is required to present a petition to the judge describing any action he proposed to take. This applies to disposal or investment of assets and to expenditures for care of the assets or for support of the incompetent and his legal dependents. The petition further indicates why the proposed action is necessary or advisable. If the judge finds the proposal acceptable, he signs a written order authorizing it. In matters pertaining to real estate, the procedural requirements are usually more detailed and incorporates more safeguards than those pertaining to personal property. In some states, the guardians act at their own discretion without court authorization, but justify their actions at the time of filing their accounts.

At the end of the first year of guardianship, the guardian prepares in writing an account referring back to the inventory to reflect his transactions. This contains a statement of receipts, including income and proceeds from any sale of disbursements made, supported by vouchers, and of the balance of cash and other assets on hand. This account is signed and sworn to by the guardian and presented to the judge for inspection and approval. It is then filed with the clerk of the court. Similar accounts are filed at the end of each succeeding year; each annual account referred back to the preceding one.

Little was spelled out in the law concerning the guardian's duties toward the incompetent as a person. Apparently it was assumed the guardian had the personal welfare of the incompetent at heart and would see that he was properly cared for. Furthermore, at the time the law of guardianship developed, little could be done for an incompetent beyond seeing that he was fed and clothed and kept from harming himself or others.

Historically, it was assumed that the assets of the incompetent would not be exhausted during his lifetime and that he would not recover from his disability. Normally the estate continued until such time as the incompetent died, at which point an executor or administrator was appointed to dispose of the decedent's assets according to law. The guardian then prepared a final account and turned over the remaining assets to the executor or administrator, or to the heir or devises, as the law indicated.

If the guardian failed to perform his duties properly, several remedies would be available:

(a) He could be removed as guardian and another appointed in his place, in which event the original guardian prepared a final account and turned over the assets to the successor guardian. This remedy was available for failure to care for the incompetent properly as well as for mismanagement of assets.

(b) The guardian could be sued for the full amount of money which he misappropriated or caused the estate to lose through mismanagement.

(c) If the guardian's own assets were insufficient to pay the judgment

10

against him, then his bondsmen could be sued up to the amount of their bond.

(d) The guardian could be placed in jail for contempt of court if he failed to obey an order of the court requiring him to make an accounting or turn over assets when required to do so.

As an additional safeguard, the judge could, at any stage, appoint an attorney called a guardian-item to represent the interests of the incompetent and scrutinize the transactions of the guardian.

Roles and Functions of Persons Involved in Guardianship Proceedings

A. The Judge, Clerk and Fiduciary

Guardianships are judicial proceedings. As such, the role of the judge is clear. He is the decision maker. Likewise the role of the clerk is clear. He keeps the records and arranges for the orderly management of the court's business.

Provisions of the guardianship statutes of a given state clearly define the role of the guardian with regard to his management of assets. He acts in place of the incompetent. His role in relation to the incompetent -in acting for him- is not usually spelled out in as much detail.

The multiple nature of guardianship proceedings has made them subject to varying emphases from one state to another and sometimes even from one county to another.

Persons other than the judge, the clerk and the fiduciary are involved in guardianship proceedings. Their roles are also important though not clearly defined.

B. The Family Member

One of these persons is the "family member." The family member is usually the first to know when an older person is no longer able to manage himself adequately. Usually he is most concerned and seeks advice. He assumes responsibility for initiating appropriate procedures and bears the responsibility in selection of a fiduciary. This family member is probably the most important person in the life of the incompetent. He should receive understanding, appreciation and skilled advice from many sources- the doctor, the psychiatrist, the lawyer and the social services. He needs this kind of help to face the situation with which he is confronted and to guide him in performing his duties to the incompetent, whether for management of assets or for personal care. He may further need help to bear up under possible family dissension over the nature of assistance to the incompetent.

C. The Lawyer

The role of the lawyer is of utmost importance. It is not always well understood, even by the lawyer himself, and has undergone shifts in focus. The lawyer's obvious role is to prepare the necessary legal documents and to arrange for, and participate in, the court proceedings. This, every lawyer understands and usually performs with skill. But if a lawyer limits his role to these, he is little more than a craftman and has missed the significance of his role as counselor.

As Counselor

With the possible exception of the family doctor, the troubled family member usually consults the lawyer first. He therefore is in a key position to be of help in evaluating problems and in marshalling resources needed for an adequate solution. In earlier times, before each branch of knowledge became so extensive and so specialized, the lawyer and the judge were often the only professional persons involved. Today, it is almost impossible for a lawyer to know intimately many other areas of knowledge. Especially in metropolitan communities he cannot have personal knowledge of all the available resources and services. Beyond this, in metropolitan communities, social life tends to be concentrated in intra- professional groups with an attendant loss of cross fertilzation of ideas. All of this places a burden on the lawyer in fulfilling his function as a counselor. He must therefore become aware of ways to get the knowledge he needs.

If guardianship proceedings are used, the lawyer becomes the attorney for the guardian. He cannot be expected to act for the incompetent or for the person who first consults him unless the latter becomes guardian. Confusion about the object of a lawyer's professional allegiance leads to unfortunate misunderstandings. In his role as attorney for the guardian, the lawyer should, but unfortunately does not always, instruct the guardian in his duties and guide him in their performance. The degree of instruction and guidance required by a particular guardian will depend upon his knowledge and experience.

As Guardian

A practice prevalent in many places is for a lawyer to act as both guardian and attorney for himself as guardian. This is generally inadvisable and even undesirable. A lawyer who acts in both capacities may sometimes fail to distinguish between the roles. He may have a tendency to over-emphasize the legal aspects of guardianship and believe quite honestly that in fulfilling the legal requirements, he is fulfilling the role. This is not always the case. Much of what a guardian should do may seem burdensome to a lawyer who would rather spend his time and energy on matters in which he has special competence. In short, many of a guardian's duties may be outside the lawyer's range of interests.

The Uniform Probate Code

A number of states have enacted statutes creating a new fiduciary concept called conservatorship, that is intended to fit the special problems of property management for the older person. These statutes were to become the prototype for conservatorship provisons in the Uniform Probate Code (UPC). It is Article V in that Code which is related to care for the affairs and property of elderly persons. The Code, has of this publication, been enacted in ten states: Alaska, Arizona, Colorado, Idaho, Minnesota, Montana, Nebraska, New Mexico, North Dakota, South Dakota, and Utah. In addition, Oregon has adopted a statute based on the UPC and is very similar to it. Maryland also has portions of Article V of the UPC, substantially modified, in its new Estates and Trusts Code.

This Code is total break with the past. But recognizing that all people are more or less sensitive to the labels put on them by other persons, one of the basic changes made by the Code is essentially semantic. The old law often required a person to be characterized either as insane or as incompetent in order for protective measures to be implemented. Unfortunately, the term incompetent has come to be equated exclusively with serious mental problems even though everyone is incompetent in some areas. An adjudication of incompetence has also become associated with appointment of guardian as well as with commitment to a mental institution. Even when a relative is truly mentally incompetent, the family dislikes the judicial adjudication of this fact and the attendant publicity. Where the relative cannot manage property, but is sufficiently competent to comprehend the guardianship proceeding, the odium of incompetence, and its unfortunate connotations, might be psychologically damaging. Furthermore, although a person may not be incompetent, as that term has come to be used, physical disability or a limited mental decline may impede that person's ability to manage his own affairs, The Code avoids these difficulties through changes in terminology. "advanced age" as well as "physical illness or disability" are now adequate bases to support a finding that a person is incapacitated for purposes of appointing a guardian of his person. These grounds are also sufficient for a finding that a person is unable to manage his property and affairs for purposes of appointing a conservator or issuing a protective order as to the person's property.

Another major change brought about by the Code is to treat the problems of care for the person, guardianship, as distinct from protection of the property, conservatorship, and within that framework to distinguish between minors and other disabled persons. The Code is flexibly designed to fit individual needs, a conservator or a guardian or both may be appointed. If both are appointed, different persons may be appointed to serve as guardian and conservator. This flexibility is useful since these positions involve different functions and call for different skills. However, the same person may serve both as guardian and conservator where, for example, the amount of property is too small to warrant professional care and a member of the family wants to act in both capacities to save costs. The court may also issue a limited protective order to authorize a single property transaction, without appointing a conservator.

. But the greatest change between the prior law and the UPC is that the conservator is treated as a trustee, with statutory powers to manage the property of the protected person as the trustee of a living trust would. He is no longer an officer of the court, exercising his powers only under court direction and supervision. Although the same fiduciary concept underlies administration of a decedent's estate, there is a difference in conservatorship because the "beneficiary" of this statutory trust is, by definition, not able to look after his own rights and to enforce the duties of the conservator-trustee. Therefore, some additional safeguards are built into the conservatorship at critical points—bonding, accounting, and judicial control over the exercise of certain major powers affecting distribution.

In short, the Uniform Probate Code is a new and emerging attempt to deal with the special issues of the older person. It presents problems as well as solutions. As time and experience may dictate, the Code may or may not replace the probate laws now prevailing in most of the states. If you are in a jurisdiction which has adopted the Code or a version of it, you will have to make a special effort to familiarize yourself with it.

Chart 1

STATES PROVIDING FOR GUARDIAN
OF THE AGED, INCOMPETENTS

State	Applicable Statutes	Power over Person	Property	Other Significant Provisions
ALA. CODE (1958)	21§9	Yes 21 §42	Yes 21 §42	Court approval needed for lease of more than one year 21 § 46. Generally management of both person & property.
ALAS. STAT. (1962)	§20:05:08	Yes §20:05.100	Yes §20:05.100	Represents ward in legal actions. Can lease property without court approval.
ARIZ. REV. STAT. (1956)	§14:863	Yes §14:863	Yes §14:963	Provides for person, property or both. Can sell property without approval. Guardian to appear, represent and sue for ward.
ARK. STAT. (Supp. 1967)	§57.605	Yes §625	Yes §626	Guardian given custody. With court approval can commit ward. Title to property remains in ward. Cannot bind ward or property. Forme contracts with court approval are valid. §628.
CAL. PROBATE CODE (West 1957)	§1460	Yes §1500	Yes §1500	Cannot have both Guardian & Conservator. §1530— Need court approval for sale of property with court approval Guardian can bind. Ward & contract for him. Also represent ward.
DEL. CODE ANN. (1953)	§12:3914	Yes 12 §3921	Yes 12 §3921	May sue in behalf of ward. Ward cannot contract away property.
FLA. STAT. ANN. (1964)	§42.744.03	Yes §744.49	Yes §§744.51, 744.52	Guardian in Florida may mean curator. Conservator or committee §744.03. Cannot bind as to property §744.49. Suits must be maintained against Guardian & ward, both.
GA. CODE ANN. (1965)	§49-601	Yes 49 §201	Yes 49 §201	Guardian same relationship as father to child. Contracts binding by court approval § 49-226.
HAWAII REV. LAWS §338		Yes §338-4	Yes §338-4	

State	Applicable Statutes	Power over Person	Property	Other Significant Provisions
IDAHO CODE (1968)	§15-1816	Yes §15-1816	Yes §15-1816	If just imcompetent to manage estate, then Guardian of estate only. §15-1816. Care & custody if required of ward. §15-1817.
IND. STAT. ANN. (1953)	§§8:106, 8:121	Yes §§8:106, 8:128	Yes §§8:106, 8:126	Guardian has custody but cannot bind. §8:129. Title in ward to property. Guardian has possession §8:130. Guardian represents estate in legal action §8-137. ward contracts are void. §:141.
IOWA CODE ANN. (1964)	32 IOWA CODE ANN. §633.556 (1964)	No	§639 Yes	Title in ward. Possession in Guardian or Conservator. Sale subject to court approval. Ward cannot dispose of property except by will if possesses testamentary capacity §638. Anyone can petition §566.
KAN. STAT. ANN. (1964)	§59.3002	Yes §3002	No	
KY. REV. STAT. (1963)	§387.060	Yes §387.060	Yes §338.060	Guardian and Committee have same powers except for education.
ME. REV. STAT. (1964)	tit. 18, §3601	Yes tit. 18, §3605	tit. 18, Yes §3505	Contracts made by ward after appointment of Guardian are void.
MASS. ANN. LAWS (1969)	201§1 201§6 (insane)	Yes 201 §12	Yes 201 §20	Contracts after appointment are void.
MICH. STAT. ANN. (1962)	§27:3178 (201)	Note: Yes for minor spendthrift or insane	Yes §27:3178 (217)	No control over person if just old age. Provision for special Guardian who has control over persons' property until appointment of General Guardian § 27:3178 (211) After appointment loses contract right 271 MICH. 215.

MINN. STAT. ANN. (1969)	§525.54	Yes §§525.54, 525.56	Yes §§525.54, 525.56	Guardian under control of court at all times. Can have General Guardian or Guardian of just the estate.
MO. STAT. ANN. (1956)	§475.030	Yes §475.120	Yes §475.130	Guardian can confine depending on degree of incompetency. §475.12. As to Real & Personal Property Guardian under court control §475.130. Contracts made by ward are invalid §475.345. But contracts made by ward with approval of Guardian & court can be binding. §475.135. Court can authorize purchase of Real Estate. §475.190.
MONT. REV. CODE (1947)	§§91-4701, 91-4702	Yes §91-4703	Yes §91-4703	
NEB. REV. STAT. (1943)	§38-201	Yes §38-202	Yes §38-202	
NEV. REV. STAT. (1963)	§159.100	No—only if ward is minor §159.250	Yes §159.250	Represent ward in legal actions §159.270.
N. H. REV. STAT. ANN. (1968)	§464.1	Yes §462.4	Yes §462.4	No contract after Guardian by ward is valid. §462.27.
N. J. STAT. ANN. (1953)	§3A:6.25	Yes §3A-6.36 (Care)	Yes §3A-6.36	Need permission of court to sell, trade, exchange, etc., property.
N. M. STAT. ANN. (1958)	§§32-2-3, 32-2-1	No provision as to custody or control.	Yes §32-2-3	Real and personal property.
N. C. GEN STAT. (1965)	§33-1	No provision (assume no custody.)	Yes §33.20	Legal Representative §33.28

State	Applicable Statutes	Power over Person	Property	Other Significant Provisions
N. D. Cent. Code Ann. (1960)	§30-10-02	Yes §30-10-14 custody	Yes §30-10-18	Isn't guardian of person or of property or both. All other guardians are special guardians §30-10-04. Provision for different guard of person & property §30-10-09.
Ohio Rev. Code Ann. (1964)	§2111.01	Yes §§2111.06, 2111.07, 2111.13	Yes §§2111.06, 2111.07, 2111.14	Assumed that Guardian will have control of both person and property unless otherwise stated by court. 43 N.E.2d 879.
Okla. Stat. Ann. (1965)	§58:851	Yes §58:853	Yes §58:853	
Ore. Rev. Stat. (1964)	§126.006	Yes §126.210	Yes §126.225	Title to property remains in ward §126.240. Guardian is legal representative §126.275. Prior contracts made by ward with court approval are valid. §126.285.
Pa. Stat. Ann. (1954)	title 50 §3301	Yes §§3102(4), 3301(a)	Yes §§3103 3401 3301(A) 3102(4)	Legal title to property remains in Ward §3103. Real and personal. Provide for temporary guardian §3301.
R. I. Gen. Laws (1957)	§33-15-8	Yes §§33-15-8, 33-15-29	Yes §§33-15-8, 33-15-19	Provider for contingent interest of Guardian vs. ward §33-15-39 (Ward or relative can apply.) Ward cannot make valid contract §33-15-44.
S. C. Code Ann. (1962)	§§37-1, 10-448, 32-1035		Yes §31-2	Judge of probate court can be the guardian. §31-102.
S. D. Code	Yes §35.1802	Yes §35.2001	Yes §35.2001	

TEX. PROBATE CODE (1956)	§114	Yes §229	Yes §230(b)	Can be for person and/or estate §34.1012. Contract powers are limited to same extent as power of minor §34.1014.
UTAH CODE ANN. (1953)	§75-13-20	Yes §75-13-31	Yes §75-13-22	Sale of property with court approval. Guardian has power over person and property unless, otherwise ordered. §75-13-30.
VT. STAT. ANN. (1959)	title 14 §§2671, 2683	Yes §2691	Yes §2691	Legal representative (a) Custody of person dependent upon the ward §2799. Contracts of ward are void. §2689.
VA. CODE (1950)	§37-1-1.32	Yes §37.1-1.38	Yes §37.1-1.42	Ownership of property is in ward. Legal representative §37.1-1.41.
WASH. REV. CODE ANN. (1967)	§11.88-100	Yes §§11.88.010, 11.92.040,	Yes §§11.88.010, 11.92.040	Both Guardian of person & Estate are under court control §11.92.010
WYO. STAT. (1957)	3-29.1	Yes §§3-29.1, 3-29.7	Yes §§3-25, 3-29.1, 3-29.7.	Legal representative §3-24
WIS. STAT. ANN. (1958)	§§319.295, 319.02, 319.12	Yes §§319.295, 319.03	Yes §§319.295, 319.03, 319.19	Temporary Guardian §319.15

Chart 2

STATES PROVIDING FOR CONSERVATORSHIP OF THE AGED, INCOMPETENTS

State	Statute	Person	Property	Other
CAL. PROBATE CODE (West Supp. 1957)	§1701	Yes §1851	Yes §1853	Conservator given care & custody of ward.
COL. REVISED STATS. (1963)	§153	No §153-9-6	Yes §153-9-6	Can ask for Conservator §153-14-13.
CONN. GEN. STAT. (1958)	Chap. 779 §45-70	Yes §45-75	Yes §45-75	Custody of ward except conservator is not the husband and ward is his wife. Temporary conservator §45-72. Need medical certificate. During pendency of issue contract and bank assets are frozen.
D. C. CODE (1967)	Chap. 15 §21:1501	Yes §21:506	Yes §21:1501	Control over person at court discretion and control over real and personal property. All transfers of real and personal property by ward during conservatorship are void §21:1507.
FLA. STAT. ANN. (1964)	42 §744.03	Yes §744.49	Yes §§744.51, 744.52, 747.19.	Curator, Conservator or Committee mean same thing as Guardian.
ILL. ANN. STAT. (1961)	3 §113	yes §121	Yes §122	Custody, while control of property is with court supervision. Conservator of estate and Conservator of person may be two different people §119. Prior contracts of ward enforceable with court permission §123. Conservator legal representative §124. Contracts made by ward void as to him §126, but other person making the contract is bound §126.

Jurisdiction			
IOWA CODE ANN. (1964)	633 §§566, 570	No	Yes §639	Title in ward. Conservator has possession. Sale of property subject to court approval. Real and personal property §640. Anyone can petition for Conservator §566. Ward cannot dispose of property except by will if he has testamentary capacity §637. After appointment of Conservator, presumption of fraud on all contracts made by ward §638.
KAN. STAT. ANN. (1964)	§59-3002	No	Yes §59-3002	
ME. REV. STAT. ANN. (1964)	tit. 18, §3701	Yes §3701	Yes §3701	
MD. ANN. CODE (1957)	16 §149	Yes §151	Yes §150	Court discretion for power over person, court supervision over real and personal property. Conservator may sue and be sued in his legal capacity.
MASS. ANN. LAWS (1969)	201 §§1, 16	No custody	Yes 201 §20	Old age specifically for Conservator. Contracts made after appointment are void.
MISS. CODE ANN. (1942)	§434.01	Yes §430.01	Yes §434.01	Conservator same powers as guardian of minor §434.05. Contract powers of conservatee are same as minor. §434.06.
N. H. REV. STAT. ANN. (1968)	§464.17	No	Yes §464.17	Conservatee must apply for Conservator.
NEB. REV. STAT. (1943)	§38-901	No	Yes §38-903	For a Conservator, Prospective Conservatee must request.
ORE. REV. STAT. (1964)	§126.626	—	Yes §126.621	

State	Provision	Person	Property	Other
R. I. GEN. LAWS (1957)	§33-15-44	No	Yes §33-15-44	Ward loses contract rights §33-15-44.
TENN. CODE ANN. (1955) HYGIENE LAW	§34-1008	No §34-1004 No custody	Yes §34-1008	Powers same as guardian of minor §34-1012, and §1008 says conservator can have custody and charge of person. Same powers as guardian of minor §1012. Contract powers of conservatee limited to same extent as minor.

TITLE				
FLA. STAT. ANN. (1964)	Committee or Curator §42.744.3	Yes §744.49	Yes §§747.19, 744.51, 747.19	Guardian shall mean same as Curator, Conservator or Committee. In addition §747.19 gives Curator specific control of property.
KY. REV. STAT. ANN. (1963)	Committee §387:210 Curator §387.320	Yes §387.230	Yes §387.320	Guardian and Committee have same power except for education of ward. Curator by petition of old age person—only control and management of real and personal property.
LA. REV. STAT. (1965)	Committee title 9:389 Curator §9:404	Yes §337	Yes §337	§406 provides for an under curator where interest of curator and ward may be in conflict. Under curatorship, persons 'act are null T.9 §401. Previous acts are also null except when conditions are notorious.
N. M. STAT. ANN. (1958)	Committee §32-21	No provision as to custody or control	Yes §32-2-3	Guardian shall include Committee.

22

				Committee subject to control of court.
N. Y. MENTAL HYGIENE LAW (McKinney Supp. 1969-70)	Committee: Mental Hygiene §100 .	Yes §100	Yes §100	
VA. CODE (1950)	Committee §§37.1-127, 37.1-132	Yes §37.1-138	Yes §37.1-132	Legal Representative §37.1-141 §37.1-127 Committee for insane or feebleminded §37.1.1(7) insane: legally incompetent because of mental disease §37.1-1(10) feebleminded—legally incompetent because of mental deficiency But committee or guardian under §37.1-132 have same powers as committee under §37.1-127 (insane or feebleminded).
W. VA. CODE (1966)	Committee §27-11-1	Yes §27-11-4 except if ward in hospital	Yes §27-11-4	Can sell property with court approval §27-11-5.
S. C. CODE OF LAWS (1962)	Committee §32-1038		Yes §32-1035	
WIS. STAT. ANN. (1958)	Committee §319.13	No	Yes §319.31	Ward must apply.
WYO. STAT. (1957)	Committee §3-29.9	§3-29.7	Yes §3-29.7	

Chapter 2

GUARDIANSHIP OF MINORS

A. Nature of Infancy

An infant, or minor, as he is often designated, is a person who because of his youthfulness is deemed by law to be incapable of handling his own affairs in his own best interest. The age 21 is generally specified by law to be the age of majority, at which time a person is presumed to have the maturity, wisdom and discretion necessary to permit him to manage for himself and to be charged with responsibility for his own acts. There are privileges, as well as disadvantages in being under age. An infant may refuse to perform a contract and the law will protect him in his refusal. He is not held responsible for wrongdoings, or torts as they are known.

A number of contingencies may advance legal majority. Marriage, in many jurisdictions, releases a female and very often male infant from disability and effects what is known as "emancipation." The social reasons for this position are

24

clear. A person who is old enough to get married and embark on a life outside the parental fold and whose interests may not necessarily coincide with those of his parents is considered old enough and wise enough to control his own person and property. Having assumed the mature status of married persons, married infants should have the powers and responsibilities of such persons. The emancipation may be partial, in that it may affect the infant's right to dispose of his personal but not his real property. Military service is another example of freedom from the disability of non-age given to persons while still under 21 years of age.

As indicated above, the laws of the various states must always be examined since emancipation may release an infant from his guardian only as to control over his person or personal property. Limitations as to his right to transfer realty, particularly in another jurisdiction, almost always continue until he is 21 years of age.

B. TYPES OF GUARDIANS

A guardian may have control over the person, the property or both of the infant. He may have the right to discipline, the duty to educate, feed and house the infant, to tend him in illness, and to provide for his recreation. In short, he may have all the duties and rights normally belonging to a parent.

Parents as Natural Guardians

Parents as natural guardians have complete control over the person and property of the child during minority. Since the child is not deemed a legal person, parents are entitled to the earnings of the child and, in some jurisdictions, the negligence of a parent may bar a child from recovering for injury done him by a third party. In most jurisdictions, the natural guardianship of a child devolves upon the father first. In the event of his death, or disability, or incapacity, the mother is considered the natural guardian. If both parents are dead or incapacitated, the grandparents become the natural guardians. A few states make both parents the natural guardians and they share responsibilities. When a child is illegitimate, the mother is the natural guardian unless she is considered morally unfit. In the case of a divorce or separation, the court decides which parent is to have custody of the child. In such cases, the other parent is permitted to visit the child and the guardianship can be changed if the child is not being properly cared for.

While the natural guardian may have control over person and property of the child, his rights are primarily over the person of the said child, and need not include control over the child's property. This is especially true where the child and parent may have conflicting property interests. On tne other hand, a legally appointed guardian generally has control over the property but not the person of an infant, particularly where the parents are alive and able to perform their own duties towards the child.

Testamentary Guardians

A person may by his will appoint a guardian for his infant children in most jurisdictions but, if the other parent survives, the guardianship will be held to apply only to the property of the infant. A sole surviving parent (i.e., a widow or widower), is permitted in most jurisdictions to name a guardian for his children in his will. This type of guardian is known as a testamentary guardian. The probate courts, or those dealing with matters of deceased persons, in general have control of such appointments. A testamentary guardian must indicate his willingness to act and in most respects is bound by the same rules as any other legally appointed guardian.

Special Guardians

When a child is removed from the custody of his natural guardian by court order, such person is called the special guardian. A special guardian is appointed very often in cases involving the infant's property where his interests may be adverse to those of his parents. A special guardian is also appointed to examine the accounts and records of a *guardian ad litem,* whose functions will be described below. As the term implies, the special guardianship is usually established for a specific purpose or in a special proceeding.

Guardian ad litem

Since a child is not a juridical person, that is, he has no standing in court, he may not sue or be sued, without a guardian. Sometimes, a guardian already appointed for other purposes may engage in litigation for the infant. Very often, a *guardian ad litem* is appointed for the purpose of litigating matters of interest to the infant. As indicated, a guardian ad litem has the duty to prosecute the action or defend it on behalf of the infant. A judgment rendered in such an action is, of course, binding on the infant and enforceable. The infant, through his guardian, has been protected in the litigation.

C. Parent-Child Relationship

A few words should be said about the legal relationship of a parent and a minor child. The parents must support and maintain a minor child and educate him according to the requirements of the law of the state. The father is entitled to the custody and control of the minor but, in the event of his death or incapacity, the mother is so entitled. It is the general rule that the father of a child under 21, as his natural guardian, is entitled to receive the earnings of the child until he attains majority. In a number of jurisdictions, in order for a parent to hold an employer liable for payment of child's wages, however, the parent must notify the employer in writing that wages should be paid directly to the parent. A parent cannot permit activities on the part of the child which may interfere with the proper education of the child. A contract for the child's services should be entered into with his parent for it to be valid.

The parents are entitled jointly to discipline the child but such discipline or punishment may not be cruel or unreasonably harsh or severe. The parent is the sole judge of the necessity and extent of parental discipline. Furthermore the parent must act in good faith and the punishment must not result from evil passions or unrestrained anger for in such latter circumstances the parent may be prosecuted even though the punishment inflicted causes no permanent injury or disfigurement to the child. The child himself, however, has no civil remedy against the parent for injuries inflicted as a result of excessive punishment.

While the parents, as we have seen, preference being given the father unless the child is of very tender years, are entitled to custody of their children, the right to such custody may be lost either voluntarily, or by behavior on the parent's part inconsistent with the welfare of the child. The right to custody, then, is not an absolute right beyond the control of the courts, and custody may be taken away from either or both parents upon a showing of unfitness. It requires a strong case, however, to induce a court to deprive the parent of custody of the child. In order to deprive a parent of the custody of his child, it must be shown that his condition in life, or his character and habits are such that provision for the child's ordinary comfort and contentment, or for his intellectual and moral development cannot reasonably be expected at the parent's hands.

The parents, or either of them, may of course relinquish custody and control over a child by voluntary contract so long as such action is not inimical to the child's best interests. However, the surrender by the parent of such right generally does not prevent his asserting it at a later date. Here, again, the best interest of the child will determine custody. The right of a parent is not lightly to be set aside and it will not be done where unfitness is not affirmatively shown or a forfeiture clearly established. Neither parent can voluntarily relinquish custody of the child so as to destroy the rights of the other parent to such custody.

A parent may recover for injuries sustained by the child due to the wrongful behavior of a third person or for loss of the child's services arising out of such wrongful action. However, where a parent sues for loss of services arising from an injury received by his infant child, damages will not be recoverable if the evidence shows that the child's own negligence was the proximate cause of the injury. It is an equally well established rule of law that if the conduct of the party causing injury to the infant is so deliberate, persistent, and intentional as to be equivalent in law to positive and wilful injury then any contributory negligence by the child will not avoid damages being assessed against the wrongdoer.

Where a parent consents to his child's being employed in a dangerous vocation, such parent assumes the risks of the employment and no recovery can be obtained in the event of subsequent injury arising out of the dangerous employment.

It is possible for a child to act as the parent's agent and where a parent permits his child to act as his agent then everything done by the child within the scope of an agent's authority will be binding upon the parent.

It is the general rule that the parent is not liable for mischief of the child, such acts of mischief being unknown to the parent and not encouraged or consented to by him in any manner. In order to be unknown to the parent the acts complained of must not, of course, be committed in the parent's presence, and in some jurisdictions the parent must show affirmatively that the child has been given a good upbringing and therefore the parent could not have anticipated the acts complained about.

D. APPOINTMENT AND SELECTION OF GUARDIANS

Generally a court will not appoint one person guardian of the child's person and another guardian of the child's property although, in exceptional circumstances, separate guardians of the person and estate of the child may be appointed. No general guardian can be appointed by a court for a child whose natural guardian is living unless such natural guardian consents to the appointment or unless the natural guardian is adjudged to be unfit or incapacitated; neither has any court the power to appoint a guardian over an individual who is not an idiot or lunatic or otherwise incompetent. Such an individual, if incapacitated from transacting business, would doubtless have the right to apply on his own behalf for appointment of a guardian for himself.

However, where a child has been placed in a charitable institution by its natural guardian, it has been held that the probate court may appoint a guardian of the person and property of such child.

The courts which generally have the power to appoint guardians of children are the probate courts or courts having probate powers though not themselves probate courts. The jurisdiction to appoint a guardian varies however from state to state; sometimes courts of equity have full power along with the probate courts and in some states juvenile courts have been given power to appoint a guardian. Where there is likelihood of a lengthy proceeding before the court, or where there are circumstances amounting to an emergency, a probate court may appoint a temporary guardian of the child until a final determination can be made as to the appointment of a general guardian.

To appoint a general guardian for a child, most states require that the child have its legal residence within the state, otherwise the court does not possess the required jurisdiction. The court may, of course, appoint a guardian for the special purpose of administering assets of the infant within the state even though said infant legally resides outside the court's jurisdiction. A very few courts, however, have stated that the mere presence of a child within the state is sufficient to give the court jurisdiction over him and consequently that a guardian may be appointed even though it is conceded that the child's legal residence is in another state. Courts following this reasoning, of course, apply the rule that a court has no jurisdiction to appoint a guardian of infants absent from the state even though their legal residence be within it. All courts try to adhere to the principle of exercising their jurisdiction for the good of the child.

Nomination by Child

Many states have enacted legislation which gives children who have attained the age of fourteen the privilege of selecting their own guardian (nomination, is the term generally used for the selection). Such guardianship is subject to the approval of the court but the court can object to the child's selection only on the ground of unfitness. In Louisiana it is required that the decision of members of the infant's family be obtained before a general guardian can be appointed for an infant upon the death or incapacitation of his natural guardian. The Louisiana courts are bound by the selection of the family meeting in the appointment of the guardian unless the selection is made in obvious bad faith, or unless the person selected is incapacitated or incompetent.

Courts will consider the wishes of the child in the selection of his guardian where the child is mature enough to arrive at an intelligent decision. As has been pointed out above, in many states a child over the age of 14 years has an absolute right to select a fit person as his guardian. Likewise a court will consider the clearly expressed views of a deceased parent in the selection of a general guardian. Other things that will be considered along with those mentioned are family ties, wishes of other members of the family, religious preference, education and age of the proposed guardian. In Louisiana certain classes of persons have been set out as having first claim on being appointed as guardian. In some states corporations have been given special rights in their charters to act as guardians; even banks and trust companies have been held competent to act as guardians in certain states.

Institutions as Guardians

The courts recognize that commercial banks have powers not vested in savings banks. Business banks are chartered by both the state and nation. They may now serve as guardian, receiver and trustee. It has been held, however, that a business partnership cannot be appointed as a guardian.

Other Factors Affecting Eligibility as Guardian

In the case of a father who is himself a minor, if he is competent to handle business affairs, the fact of his minority in some states will not be a bar to his being appointed guardian of his child. In all other situations a minor will generally not be appointed as guardian. Married women and strangers to the child are not barred by reason of such status from being appointed as guardians. As we have pointed out above however, by statute and judicial decision, parents and relatives are entitled to priority in consideration by the court for appointment as guardians. Also the nearness in the blood relationship is a factor to be taken into consideration with the closeness of degree of kinship to be favored. There must be a determination of unfitness of the parent before a third person can be appointed by the court as guardian for a child. In determining the respective right of the parents, all things being equal, the right of the father is generally stronger than that of the mother unless the child is of a very young age. A parent by virtue of adoption obtains most but not all the rights of a natural parent. According to the Louisiana courts, the child's grandmother was entitled to appointment as guardian in preference to an aunt who adopted the child with the father's consent during his lifetime. However, in Kansas, the courts have held that the relationship created by adoption gave the same right of custody as natural parentage. The latter view is held by the majority of courts.

Some courts, deciding in line with the father's superior right of custody give the superior right of custody to relatives on the father's side. Other courts have held that paternal and maternal relatives are equal in right to custody. The courts are about equally divided on this point, generally deciding in favor of the relative best able to care for the child. In general, it may be said that courts are inclined to be guided by the moral character of the person seeking to be appointed guardian and will select that person who seems best able to advance and promote the interests of the infant.

Some states by statute forbid the appointment of the executor or administrator of the parent's estate as guardian of the minor children. Even, in the absence of statutory prohibition such individuals are almost never appointed as guardians because of the possibility of conflict of interests which would arise from one individual serving in such dual capacity. It should be remembered that the appointment of a general guardian for a child is a judicial proceeding and the requirements of the statute authorizing such appointment must be observed. Some statutes require notice to be given to interested parties of proceedings being brought for the appointment of a guardian; other statutes require no notice whatsoever. Most statutes provide, where proceedings are brought to have a third party appointed as guardian of a child, that the parents receive notice of the proceedings.

Most courts will presume that a parent is a fit person for guarding the welfare of his minor child so that it is necessary to show by positive evidence that such parent is unfit to be the guardian. Such evidence may take the form of proof showing, among other things, moral or physical unfitness; failure to provide for the child; testimony in divorce cases as to desertion or moral turpitude on the part of the parent; mental incompetence; unfitness of the place in which the child is being reared; drunkenness or excessive use of drugs by the parent.

Generally an appeal will not be allowed from an order which decides on the appointment of a guardian for a child unless the statute in the particular state specifically provides for such an appeal being taken to a higher court. Where the statute permits an appeal ordinarily any person interested in the proceedings who has suffered an adverse decision in the lower court may appeal.

E. COURT SUPERVISION OF GUARDIAN

The court exercises close supervision over the actions of the guardian and generally it may be said, that a guardian needs the court's authorization to inflict corporal punishment on the ward; to train the ward in a specified profession when his parents had not consented thereto; to sell or mortgage real property; to confine the ward in an institution; to invest in other than approved securities; to withdraw from investment any capital already invested and yielding a return; to lend or borrow money; to accept inheritances without inventory or to refuse inheritances; to incur extraordinary expenses; to commence litigation; to take appeals and to settle or compromise claims. It should not be assumed from the above that those matters listed are the only ones in which the guardian is supervised and controlled by the court, as the guardian is subject to the control and direction of the court at all times and in all matters.

Obligations of Guardian

In addition, the guardian has certain definite obligations toward his ward in that he must prosecute and defend law suits for his ward when necessary; sell assets when the interests of the ward and his estate so require; pay reasonable charges for the support, maintenance and education of the ward in surroundings suitable to the ward's station in life; pay debts of the ward and reasonable charges incurred for the support, maintenance, and education of his family; possess and manage the estate; collect all debts and claims and invest all funds in such securities as are proper for investment of trust funds.

Since the property of the ward is held primarily for the support, maintenance and education of the ward, it is generally necessary to obtain the approval of the court for expenditures on behalf of the ward's family. Likewise the guardian usually needs the court's permission to continue a business on behalf of the ward and to mortgage or lease real estate owned by the ward.

Guardian Accounting to Court

The guardian, furthermore, is required to file with the court periodic accountings or returns showing the status of the guardianship. Sometimes this is on a calendar basis; sometimes at the discretion of the court, and many states have fairly complicated statutory requirements with respect to these returns. For a detailed picture of the requirements in all 48 states see chart in the appendix.

F.   CARE OF THE WARD'S PERSON

The only parties entitled to the custody of a minor child, with the exception of institutions in which children have been legally placed, are the natural parents. In order for the natural parents to be deprived of custody we have seen that there must be a judicial determination of unfitness or a voluntary giving up of custody on their part. Adoptive parents stand, for the purpose of this discussion, in the same place as natural parents. When, as a result of lawful appointment, a general guardian is placed in charge of a ward such guardian owes to the ward the same duty of care and custody as the ward's natural parents.

The guardian has the duty to support the infant-ward and educate him in a manner suitable to the ward's financial and social station in life. The guardian, however, is not compelled to maintain the ward out of his own monies but may use the ward's funds for this purpose. This is the primary distinction between a guardian and an adoptive parent. The adoptive parent must maintain and educate the child at the adoptive parent's expense.

It is the rule that the guardian may pay whatever are necessary expenses for the maintenance and education of the ward from the income, *not the principal,* of the ward's estate. Where the circumstances are such that the income is insufficient to maintain the ward properly and expenditure of the principal may be necessary, then the guardian should obtain the advice and consent of the court in advance of such expediture of principal.

However, in the case of a testamentary guardian, where the will from which the ward's funds are derived authorizes the expenditure of principal on his behalf, such expenditure is proper if reasonable in amount and for a necessary purpose.

Where the expenditure involved is of income only, the question of necessity is left largely to the guardian's judgment. The guardian must act in good faith and with the prudence of the ordinary reasonable man in making such expenditures, otherwise he will be held liable to the ward's estate upon the accounting.

Where the guardian, as an individual, adopts the minor ward, then such guardian stands in the same relationship toward such child as a parent and is legally liable for maintainance and education from the date of adoption. However, the mere fact of taking the ward into the guardian's family and bringing such child up together with the guardian's own family is not enough to show an intention on the part of the guardian to adopt and, therefore, ordinarily, reimbursement to the guardian for expenses incurred on behalf of the ward will be allowed under these circumstances.

Where the father, the natural guardian of the child, has

also been appointed special guardian of an estate left the child, such father being under a legal duty to support, educate and maintain his child, cannot reimburse himself out of the child's estate for the expenses of support and education. Where such father is financially unable to support the child a showing to this effect will obtain the court's permission to use part of the child's funds for this purpose.

The courts have generally held the mother not to be liable to the same extent as the father for the support of a minor child and have been more lenient in allowing a mother reasonable reimbursement out of the child's separate estate for expenses incurred by her in the support and maintenance of her child. Where the mother derives benefit from the child's services, however, courts have been reluctant to allow her reimbursement out of the child's separate estate for maintenance and support.

The guardian may properly expend the ward's income for food, lodging, clothing, medicine and other necessaries suitable to the ward's station in life. Here, again the paramount consideration is the child's welfare; also what may be necessary for one ward may not be for another in different circumstances. The test is whether the guardian has safeguarded the ward's interests and taken care of him as a reasonable, prudent man would have done. The facts of each particular case are different and the courts do not attempt to maintain hard and fast rules as to what is necessary and what is not.

Where a guardian permits a ward to live beyond his means and where expenditures are extravagant then the guardian will be held personally responsible for the excesses.

Where expenses may be by nature rather large in amount, such as, for example, in connection with fees for college enrollment and maintenance then the question is usually for the court to decide and the guardian should obtain an order covering the question. The guardian should, however, pay all necessary and reasonable expenses in connection with attendance at grade school.

G. CARE OF THE WARD'S PROPERTY

It is the general rule of law that the duly appointed general guardian represents the ward in all business transactions and litigation. The guardian represents the ward in somewhat the same fashion that the executor of a will represents the testator and the legatees. The guardian may release signatories on notes or mortgages or other instruments of indebtedness but such releases must not be devoid of consideration and, of course, cannot be harmful to the ward's interests. Any fraudulent acts of such guardian will be sufficient to effect his dismissal as guardian by the supervising court and to render the guardian liable to the infant's estate for the loss resulting. Any unauthorized or improper release of security or extension of time for payment of obligations due the ward's estate will not be binding and will not be validated by the court. Therefore, those conducting business with a guardian are obliged to examine his authority for the proposed action since they know that the guardian is dealing with the funds and property of his wards; such persons are also charged with the knowledge that the guardian's powers and duties are strictly controlled by statute. The guardian's authority to act can, of course, be relied upon where it is shown that the court has duly authorized the action. It has been said that one dealing with a guardian must use reasonable diligence and prudence to ascertain whether the guardian acts within the scope of his powers. Lacking express authorization a guardian does not have any right to carry on a business enterprise on behalf of the ward. This is so even where the business is the continuance of that of the testator of the will from which the ward derives his estate.

Compromise of the Ward's Claims

Unless the statute involved specifically prohibits the guardian from compromising or settling claims due his ward, a general guardian is permitted to do so but he must act with reasonable prudence, which we have seen is the judgment of a reasonable man under the circumstances. Most courts do not require approval before the settlement, but in cases where there may be some doubt as to the

37

propriety of settlement a cautious guardian will most certainly protect himself by obtaining court approval respecting the settlement or compromise proposed. When such approval has been obtained the guardian is protected by law; in the absence of such approval his action remains open to challenge. Where the guardian secures court approval in advance of compromise, such settlement may not later be questioned, unless fraud is uncovered at a later date. If such approval is not obtained in advance, then the guardian's judgment is later open to question. By that time, circumstances may have changed completely, (as for example, the value of securities or real estate may have radically changed) and the guardian may find himself in a highly disadvantageous position.

As we have noted above, some states by statute prohibit a compromise or settlement by the guardian without consent of the court. A settlement, in the face of such a statute, where prior court approval has not been obtained is deemed void.

Where it can be shown that a settlement by a guardian although approved by the court was in fact improvident or fraudulent then it is proper to commence a proceeding in the same court to vacate or set aside the order approving the settlement.

In the states of Connecticut, Georgia and Kentucky a distinction is made between a *claim* and a *debt,* the distinction being that a *claim* is still in dispute and no fixed amount has been determined as to the value of the claim, while a *debt* represents a sum certain.

It is recognized that a general guardian has complete power over the personal estate of his ward and is entitled to possession of it, but some courts hold that such guardian has no power over the real estate belonging to the ward other than to see that it is profitably leased and maintained and rents are collected. According to this view the guardian is not entitled to possession of the ward's realty.

In some states legislation is in force which limits the right of even the natural guardian to possession and supervision over his child's estate. (Florida, New York, Tennessee.)

While the guardian has possession of the ward's personal estate and control over his real estate the title to such property remains in the ward and the guardian is deemed to be a trustee. As we have seen above it is the duty of the guardian to exercise the highest good faith on his ward's behalf and to protect the ward in every reasonable manner and his acts are scrutinized carefully by the courts.

Guardian's duty to conserve

It is the duty of the guardian to conserve and protect the ward's estate in every way. While the guardian is in fact a trustee of the ward's property, it has been stated that the courts require a more jealous guarding of the interests of such helpless persons (wards) than those of other beneficiaries of trusts. A guardian has the right to rely on the advice of experts or professional persons chosen carefully for any special work that may be necessary in connection with matters arising out of the ward's estate, and is not liable for mistakes made by such experts.

The guardian must collect all debts due the ward's estate and is under duty to institute such litigation as may be necessary to obtain possession of the ward's real estate or other assets that may wrongfully be in the hands of others.

Care of Ward's real property

While the guardian is generally permitted to lease the real property of the ward without court permission, the lease should not extend either beyond the term of the guardianship or beyond the date of the ward's minority. Also the lease should be in the usual form used in the area where the property is located and should be on terms which are in compliance with the state statutes in all respects and which obtain the best bargain available on behalf of the ward. Where land or buildings belonging to the ward are vacant, the guardian is under a duty to lease them as quickly as possible on the best terms available in order to realize income on the ward's estate. Failure to do this, arising out of negligence on the guardian's part, will cause the guardian to be held liable for any loss which

39

the ward's estate may sustain as a result of such failure. The guardian is under a duty, furthermore, to maintain the real estate of his ward in such fashion as to prevent any violations of municipal or other ordinances from attaching to it and as we have seen a guardian has no right to mortgage the ward's realty without prior court authorization. It is, also, the general rule that a guardian may not pledge or borrow upon securities or personal property of the ward without first obtaining court approval. Likewise, the guardian has no right to sell or contract for the sale of the ward's realty without full court approval of the terms of the proposed sale unless the statute under which the guardian is appointed confers such power. Where the statute confers such power to the guardian then strict compliance with its terms and conditions is necessary; usually such authority is granted only for the purposes of maintenance and education of the ward or in a partition proceeding—that is where the ward owns an undivided interest in the land. The guardian may also derive such authority to sell from the will appointing him guardian; but authority conferred upon a testamentary guardian cannot violate statutory provisions and requirements.

Sale of ward's assets

Provided there is not any statutory prohibition, it is the general rule of law that the guardian is permitted to sell the personal assets of the ward without court authorization. This is only logical and practical as securities and similar personal assets of the ward's estate are of such a nature that the guardian should be free to use his discretion in the investment and reinvestment thereof as the economic situation changes. However, where there is no court order directing the guardian to sell securities forming part of the ward's estate, failure to sell them and a future decline in their value will not make the guardian liable for the loss in the absence of a showing of fraudulent conduct or imprudence on his part.

We have observed that it is the duty of the guardian to keep the lands and buildings of the ward leased for the best possible rental in order to derive income to the estate;

so it is the guardian's duty likewise, to keep the funds of the ward invested in income bearing securities approved by the state or the court for the investment of trust funds or in other types of prudent investment. The courts are insistent upon the guardian's adhering to the letter of the law in this respect, and the investment of such funds must be in the name of the ward. Where the guardian is in doubt as to his authority regarding any particular investment he should apply to the court for direction.

It is important that the guardian consult the court beforehand rather than ask for mere ratification after the act, as many court decisions hold that where the statute provides that proposed investments shall first be passed upon by the court before they are made, the court is without power to ratify investments after they are made. The general rule is that the court can specially authorize a guardian to make an investment of the ward's funds in securities which are not among those listed by general statutes regulating the estates of wards. This is true, also, under provisions of the Uniform Veterans' Guardianship Act. The guardian is of course, under all conditions required to give prudent consideration to the security behind the proposed investment, the ease with which it may be converted to cash if the need arises, and the rate of return. As we have already seen generally, the guardian is here again bound to use the utmost good faith, and the care and prudence which the ordinary, reasonable man uses in the conduct of his business. Where, because of changing conditions, the character of the investment changes and the guardian has knowledge of probable depreciation in the security the guardian has the duty of changing the investment, if possible; otherwise he may be held liable for the resultant loss due to his negligence.

The courts do not go so far as to regard the guardian as an insurer of the investment but they do insist upon his observing the particular statutory requirement restricting his investments on behalf of his ward and his acting with the highest degree of fidelity to his trust and exerting the utmost prudence in his choice of investment.

Guardian's duty to convert assets of ward

The guardian is, furthermore, under the obligation of converting nonlegal investments in the ward's estate into approved investments. (Legal investments are those approved for savings banks, trustees of estates and others in similar positions of trust, and include only the most conservative securities where the return may be only moderate but almost always sure.) He must use his discretion and best judgment as to the appropriate time for changing such investments so as to realize as much as possible; he must not retain such nonlegal investments beyond a reasonable time, however, and when in doubt as to their disposal he should make an application to the court for directions regarding their retention.

The guardian may purchase real estate with the funds of the ward only with court or statutory approval. It is the general rule that the guardian must justify such purchase with facts to show its necessity. It is the majority view that an unauthorized purchase of real estate by the guardian is voidable by the ward when he attains his majority, but the Missouri cases hold such unauthorized purchases absolutely void. It is the duty of the general guardian to deposit the ward's funds in a bank while such funds are uninvested. The guardian must employ good faith and reasonable diligence in the selection of such depository. Here, again, the rule is that the guardian is not an insurer of the funds, but his conduct is to be tested by the exercise of reasonable prudence. The selection of a solvent private banker by the guardian rather than an incorporated bank under the supervision of the state superintendent of banks is permissible. Some courts designate the bank in which the funds are to be deposited, while in other state, by statute, the court may direct the guardian to withdraw the funds from a failing or insolvent institution and deposit them in some solvent bank but cannot designate a particular bank as the depository. As we have seen, deposits by a guardian must be in the name of the ward's estate and where the guardian fails to deposit such funds in the name of the ward's estate and there is nothing to indicate that the deposit is made in a representative capacity, as guardian, then such guardian is liable to the ward where the fund was lost through failure of the bank without regard to the guardian's good faith or his intention when making the deposit.

Guardian's Duty to Invest Funds

Where the ward's funds are temporarily deposited in the bank, while awaiting investment, and no showing is made that such funds were needed for current expenses of the ward and the guardian makes no attempt to invest the funds within a reasonable time then the guardian will be liable for the loss of such funds, due to the bank's becoming insolvent and the guardian and surety will, likewise, be liable for interest on such monies from the date of the bank's insolvency.

As we have noted before, the guardian is required to exercise reasonable diligence to keep the funds of the ward invested. He may not keep idle the money or property of his ward but is under a duty to keep the money invested in good securities and must exercise reasonable diligence to keep it so invested at all times and if he fails to do so he will be charged by the court with a reasonable rate of interest for the use of the money during the period it might have been invested. Likewise, where the guardian keeps the ward's money in his hands and does not pay it out to the ward when the latter becomes of age, then such guardian is liable for interest on such funds and in addition thereto the statutory penalty, if any.

The guardian is generally chargeable with interest at the highest legal rate allowed by law in the particular state where the case is one involving misuse of his ward's funds; however, where the guardian has merely failed to invest the money of his ward and has made no personal use of it, then his liability will generally be for interest only at the rate which the money would have earned. In a few cases courts have charged the guardian with compound interest in situations where the guardian has misappropriated his ward's funds or unlawfully loaned money to a corporation in which the guardian was himself financially interested.

As we have already pointed out, the guardian must keep

the ward's real estate in suitable repair and will be entitled to reasonable expenses in this connection. A court order for such expenditures is generally not necessary unless the expenditures are for remodeling of a building or for extraordinary repairs. The guardian must moreover obtain a court order to permit him to place improvements on otherwise unimproved lands of the ward.

Guardian's Right to Employ Help

The guardian is entitled to employ, where necessary and for reasonable compensation, the services of agents and others in order to manage and maintain the ward's estate. Likewise a guardian is entitled to employ attorneys, where necessary, to conduct litigation on behalf of the ward and the guardian is entitled to make reasonable disbursements out of the ward's estate in payment of counsel fees and expenses incident to the trial of law-suits. However, it is not a proper expenditure for the guardian to pay out of the ward's estate for services of an attorney rendered to the guardian in a contest between the guardian and his ward for the purpose of defeating legal and substantial rights of his ward.

Guardian's Duty Not to Profit from Infant

Under no circumstances will the guardian be permitted to reap personal benefit from the estate of the ward other than reasonable compensation for services on behalf of such estate. The office of the guardian being one of trust and obligation he is under a duty to act for the best interest of his ward and not his own and it is the clear legal duty of the guardian to keep separate all guardianship funds and not to commingle them with his own individual property. The guardian cannot lend his ward's funds to himself or put up as collateral any of the ward's estate as security for a loan to himself.

Where there is a conflict of interest between the guardian and his ward the proper course for the guardian to pursue is to resign forthwith. Where the guardian has a vital interest which is adverse to that of the ward any consent by the guardian to a settlement or compromise will be invalid insofar as the ward is concerned. By the same rule it is improper for the guardian to invest any of the ward's money in the guardian's business or property.

Since the test of a guardian's management of the ward's estate is what the ordinary prudent, reasonable man would do under similar circumstances it may be the duty of the guardian under certain circumstances to insure the property of the ward against fire, loss, or theft; and where such insurance would be proper a guardian who fails to so insure can be held liable for waste of guardianship property in the event of loss or destruction.

H. DISPOSAL OF WARD'S PROPERTY

The disposal of the ward's property by the guardian by means of sale or otherwise is closely controlled by the courts pursuant to statutory provisions in the great majority of states. Some statutes go into great detail to describe the circumstances under which it is proper to sell the ward's estate either in whole or in part; where the statute is of a general nature, however, or where there is no statutory regulation then the court has discretion to decide the circumstances that make a sale of the ward's property advisable. After sale of all or part of the ward's estate the guardian under direction of the court may be authorized to invest the ward's funds in other property.

Where a statute authorizes the sale of a ward's real estate when necessary the guardian acting under direction of the court is empowered to exchange the ward's land for other land if such exchange is a desirable transaction from the point of view of the ward's interests. Generally the court situated in the place where the land is located is the proper court to decide the question of the sale of the land. A court in one state cannot order the sale of a ward's land located in another state.

A court has no power to authorize the guardian to sell any of the ward's property if such sale would be in contravention of conditions in the will under which the ward inherited the estate.

It was the general rule of the common law, as expressed by the English courts, that the nature of a ward's property must not be changed by the guardian, by court authorization or otherwise, so as to convert personal property into real property or real property into personal. It was also the English rule of law that in the absence of express statutory authorization there could be no conversion of the ward's property except for the purpose of paying the ward's debts or supporting and educating the ward. These principles have been carried over into the jurisprudence of many American states and although statutes in many states do permit the guardian to sell the lands of his ward for purposes other than just the payment of the ward's debts and the support and education of the ward it is the rule that, under such statutes, the guardian must strictly comply with the law granting such permission and sell the ward's property only for such purposes as are particularly specified and set forth in the statutes themselves.

Unless the authority to sell the lands of the ward exists under the statutory provisions, there is no power to sell, and the sale, whether made by order of the court or not, is void. Likewise the transaction must be an actual sale and not the mere bartering or exchange of one piece of property for another without necessity.

Even where the proposed sale is for the purpose of paying the ward's debts, such should not be ordered unless the debts are pressing and the income will not be sufficient to pay up the debts in a reasonable time. Most statutes require that in order for a sale of the ward's real estate to be valid, there must first be presented to the court a petition setting forth the reasons why the sale of such property is imperative. Such statutory requirements are mandatory and where there has not been substantial compliance the court does not acquire jurisdiction to order the guardian to sell. Likewise such statutes generally indicate what persons are to be notified of the application and proposed sale. It is particularly important that ward's property which is proposed to be sold be accurately described in the application.

As we have noted before, the law of Louisiana requires a family meeting of the ward's relatives in order to recommend the guardian to be appointed by the court; likewise in Louisiana it is necessary that a family meeting be called and approval first had and obtained from it before the guardian (or tutor as he is called in Louisiana) can dispose of the ward's property. Such family meeting must in fact decide that the sale is necessary for the ward's welfare before such sale is valid.

The guardian must manifest by evidence that it is to the advantage of the ward to sell or exchange his property before the court will enter an order or decree authorizing such sale. The court decree authorizing the guardian to sell must be in strict compliance with the statutory requirements in this respect.

Many statutes require an appraisal of the property to be sold to be furnished to the court by the guardian before such sale can be authorized. Such appraisal must be performed by competent, disinterested real estate experts.

Some statutes require a special sale bond to be furnished by the guardian in order to protect the ward's interests in connection with the sale. This is discussed further in the chapter dealing with surety bonds.

Unless authorized by statute, or by the court, where there is no statutory provision governing it, the sale of the ward's property must be at public auction by the party authorized by the court to make the sale—generally a licensed auctioneer. Usually anyone may buy the property at the sale except the guardian. After the sale has been held it is usual for the court to issue an order confirming all the details of the transaction and a deed is thereupon delivered by the guardian to the purchaser. Some statutes provide that the ward have an opportunity to redeem or buy back his property after the sale thereof; in the absence of such statutory provision the sale is final.

Where it can be shown that the statutory requirements were not complied with or that the sale was fraudulent, then an action can be brought on behalf of the ward to invalidate the sale. Such action would be commenced by means of a petition setting forth the facts addressed to the court which ordered the sale. Where the sale is set aside, the purchaser, if he has acted in good faith, is usually entitled to a refund of the purchase price and reimbursement for any taxes paid on the property.

I. ACCOUNTING ON A SALE

Upon a valid sale of the ward's property it becomes the duty of the guardian to account for the monies received by him. If the successful bidder at the sale fails to pay the full amount of his bid when it becomes time for him to do so then it is the duty of the guardian to institute suit against such purchaser for the full amount of the bid.

Where a guardian is authorized by statute or a court order to sell property he is not empowered to mortgage or hypothecate the property. Therefore, in order to have authority to mortgage or lease property the guardian must obtain the court's permission in the absence of statutory direction giving the guardian such authority.

It is also the general rule of law that authority from a court to a guardian to borrow money for the ward's estate does not give the guardian the right to hypothecate or pledge assets of the estate as security for the money borrowed.

Where the statutes give the guardian the right to mortgage or pledge the ward's property pursuant to direction of the court it is usual that such statutes specify the purposes for which the estate may be mortgaged. The statutory limitations are generally to the effect that it must be necessary for the support and education of the ward, or for payment of the ward's debts, or to pay off an existing mortgage and obtain one on terms more favorable to the ward's interests.

Likewise, some statutes limit the term for which the guardian may lease the lands belonging to the ward.

Many statutes require that the guardian obtain the court's permission to mortgage real estate by means of a proceeding similar to that required for the sale of the ward's real property. Here again the statutory provisions must be strictly complied with in order for the guardian's actions to be sustained.

J. ACCOUNTING AND SETTLEMENT

The duty to account for every administrative act or failure to act rests upon the guardian as it does upon any trustee administering an estate or fund. The accounting may be defined for the scope of this discussion as a statement in writing, sworn to as to veracity, containing in full detail all the data concerning every financial transaction entered into by the guardian with the ward's funds. It contains a full disclosure of the guardian's dealings as guardian with the debtors to, the creditors of, and any persons interested in, the ward's estate, together with a complete statement showing every receipt and disbursement and itemizing every expense. All items should be appropriately grouped in schedules.

The accounting is a special proceeding in the court whereby the account itself is subjected to the court's judicial scrutiny. Such examination by the court need not always take form of a final determination. There may, in other words, be intermediate accountings by the guardian. If it does take the form of a final judicial determination then the account is said to be judicially settled.

As will be noted by consulting the appropriate chart in the appendix, most state statutes require various intermediate accountings in the form of annual returns or otherwise. These accountings are intended, generally, to be informatory, and settlement is not contemplated. Those accountings, including the final settlement, which are required either by statute or by the court are generally termed *compulsory accounts*. The guardian may, of course, from time to time submit *voluntary accounts* which as the name indicates are those accounts given to the court without compulsion as information regarding the status of the ward's estate.

Annual accounts which are passed upon by the court and judicially settled become final as to those payments made and as to the time involved.

Time of accounting

There are certain situations where the guardian may, either by virtue of statutory provision or the court's discretion, be compelled to submit his account for judicial settlement. These situations include demand for a judicial settlement by the ward after he has attained his majority; the death of the ward and the subsequent filing of a pe-

49

tition by the ward's executor or administrator asking for settlement of the ward's estate; where the guardian has been removed, demand by his successor that the removed guardian account for the period of his guardianship; and likewise because of the request of the surety on the guardian's bond. In each of the above instances and in any other where it is sought to compel the guardian to account, the procedure is to petition the court to compel the accounting. The petition, as we have seen in other instances, must conform to the statutory requirements as to form and sufficiency.

Where the guardian himself seeks a judicial settlement of his account, he should present to the court a written petition, duly verified, asking for a judicial settlement of his account and a discharge from his duties and liabilities. Those persons who, by statute, or by the court's direction are to be given notice of the proceeding, must be given whatever notice is required.

Accounting and settlement procedure is generally the same whether the guardian be a general guardian appointed by the court or a guardian named in a will or deed.

Objections may be filed by any interested party to any item in the guardian's account as filed and it is immaterial whether the account is compulsory or voluntary, whether an interim accounting or a final settlement, and whether the entire account is contested or only one item in the account. The way to secure a judicial determination is to file an objection to the disputed account or part thereof. The controversy is then determined upon a trial.

Where upon the final settlement it appears that the general guardian has expended upon the ward all the ward's property and more besides, then the final decree will show the ward to be indebted to the guardian and the latter can then take the necessary proceedings to enforce his claim against the ward.

When the guardian's authority has been revoked by the court the guardian may then present to the court a written petition, duly verified, asking that his account be judicially settled. This is generally taken care of by the court because in revoking the guardian's authority the court will generally direct him to settle his account forthwith.

It is to be advised that every account which will receive judicial scrutiny be prepared with the thought that interested parties may put in an objection either to the whole account or part thereof. It is the duty of the guardian to keep his books in a businesslike fashion and to keep proper books of account; it is likewise the duty of the guardian to prepare his own account or have it prepared at his personal expense unless he can show that the size of the estate is such that it is necessary to employ expert accountants to prepare it. Expenditure for expert accountants will be allowed only in exceptional cases.

Where the guardian can show justification for it, expenses involved in having a bookkeeper tend to the books of account will be allowed to be charged to the ward's estate.

In the preparation of the account the guardian should see to it that the account shall be a complete one and shall include all matters with which he is chargeable in his capacity as guardian. The guardian should bear in mind also that he must account for all the assets of the ward's estate which have formed a part of the guardianship trust. It is generally required that there be attached to the statement of accounts the guardian's affidavit stating that the account contains, according to the best of his knowledge and belief, a full and true statement of all his receipts and disbursements on behalf of the ward, and of all money or property belonging to the ward which has come into the guardian's hands, or has been received by any other person, by virtue of the guardian's order or authority, for his use, and that the guardian does not know of any error or omission in the account. The guardian should submit along with the account all vouchers for payments and disbursements made.

K. Removal of the Guardian

It is the general rule that in order to remove a guardian the grounds upon which such application is based must be specified in the statute governing the situation of a guardian deemed unsuitable for the position entrusted to him. In the absence of statutory rules for removal, the courts have decided for themselves the fitness of the guardian upon the circumstances before the courts.

Inasmuch as each state statute differs it is impossible to set out within the scope of this work all the reasons which have been found sufficient cause for removal, but the major grounds may be stated to be: fraud in appointment; failure to discharge duties; abuse of powers; insanity or incompetence; habitual drunkenness; failure to comply with an order of the court; failure to make returns or schedules or to produce assets; waste, corruption, embezzlement, or mismanagement; failure to give bond or security as required; conviction of a felony; appointment of a receiver for a corporate guardian; neglect of the ward's person or property; guardian becoming a non-resident of the state of his appointment; improper investment of the ward's money; speculating with or commingling the ward's funds; failure to account and settle as provided by statute or the court.

Removal of a guardian is accomplished by a petition to the appointing court asking for such removal. Any interested person may start such proceeding by means of a petition either as a friend on behalf of the infant ward, or the court itself may institute such proceedings upon the facts being brought to its attention. Any statutory requirements with respect to the form and sufficiency of the petition and the facts to be alleged therein must of course be complied with in order for the removal petition to be considered by the court. In almost all cases the court which appointed the guardian has the power to remove him but here again any pertinent statutory requirements must be followed. The petitioning party, naturally has the burden of proving the unfitness of the guardian as alleged in the petition and the guardian must be given the opportunity to defend himself against the charges. The court has great discretion in considering what shall be done with respect to removal and generally considers of paramount importance the effect which removal will have upon the welfare of the ward. This is the most important consideration before the court. While the proceeding for removal is in the process of being heard before the court it is proper for the court to enjoin the guardian temporarily from acting in such capacity until a final decision has been rendered. Where a guardian is removed for unfitness or other cause as alleged in the petition it is appropriate for him to be charged personally with the costs of the proceeding. This, again, lies largely within the discretion of the court.

With respect to the voluntary resignation of, or withdrawal by the guardian this, too, must be approved by the court which must be satisfied that the guardianship affairs are in order before the resignation will be accepted and the guardian discharged. The guardian remains liable for the ward's affairs until an order of discharge has been made by the court.

Chapter 3

SPECIAL TOPICS IN THE
GUARDIAN-MINOR RELATIONSHIP

A. Rights of Guardian Against Infant Ward

The ordinary position of a parent or of a guardian to a minor is that such person cannot sue the child or the ward. A right of action at law is not open to any and all persons against all others, without reference to relationships which may exist between them. It is the general rule, then, that a guardian, or one standing in the place of a parent, cannot sue his ward, because committed as he is to the care and protection of the ward's interests, going to law with the ward to recover a judgment against him is precluded as inconsistent. The character of the relationship, the capacity in which the guardian acts, and his duty to the ward's property forbid that they should occupy the distinctly adverse position of suitors at law, especially as to transactions occurring since the guardianship commenced. One person cannot, at the same time, occupy the position of parent or guardian, fulfilling the functions devolving upon that position, and the position of plaintiff demanding damages from the child at law.

B. Rights of Infant Against Guardian

During the term of the guardianship the ward cannot sue the guardian, but upon attainment of legal age, or upon a final accounting by the guardian, the ward may sue his guardian or former guardian; and likewise in the case of a deceased guardian the ward can maintain suit against the estate.

C. Actions by and Against Infant Wards During Guardianship

Some state statutes expressly authorize the guardian to maintain suit in the ward's name to protect his ward's interests but even in the absence of statutory authorization on this point the guardian has the duty during the term of the guardianship to institute suit on behalf of the ward in proper cases and to defend the ward's interests where necessary. It should also be here noted that the statutes sometimes provide which courts shall have jurisdiction over litigation involving guardianship matters. In the absence of specific allocation of jurisdiction the probate court generally is the proper forum. A chart in the appendix indicates the appropriate court in each state.

The courts have generally held that while the statutes of limitation operate against the guardian, such statutes do not commence to run against the ward during his minority.

As we have noted elsewhere many statutes provide that in the event of litigation involving a ward the court shall appoint a guardian *ad litem* for the purpose of representing the ward in litigation. Some states, however, permit the general guardian to sue on behalf of the ward without appointment of another as guardian *ad litem*.

Where a guardian is suing for or defending his ward in litigation he is again held to the standard of utmost good faith and should not provoke needless litigation or, where there is no legitimate defense on behalf of the ward, the guardian should not procure attorneys to file pleadings or appear in court incurring expense to the ward's estate.

The authority of the guardian to sue and be sued on behalf of his ward is limited to the state in which he is functioning as guardian. This is true, generally, in that a guardian cannot act as such outside of the state of his appointment. In the event the ward has property or interests located outside the state of appointment it is necessary to have the courts of the other state authorize the appointment of a foreign or ancillary guardian to look after the ward's interests in that jurisdiction. The powers of such foreign or ancillary guardian are governed by the local laws although such ancillary guardian is generally subject to some control and supervision by the general guardian.

Claims of third persons against the estate of the ward frequently arise where the ward has been supplied with necessaries without a specific contract with the guardian. It is the general rule of law that unless there was an explicit or implied agreement with the guardian a third person who supplies support or maintenance to a ward acquires no enforceable claim against the guardian or the ward's estate. However the estate of the ward is ultimately liable for necessities furnished for the support and care of the ward and generally the probate court, which under most statutes has the power to pass upon and allow or disallow such third party claims, will order payment of such claims where the facts establish that the goods furnished were necessary for the ward and where there is no showing of fraud or collusion.

D. GUARDIAN'S BOND

Generally, by statute, a guardian is compelled to post a bond as a guarantee of performance of his duties. The object of a bond is to afford security to those who are interested in the property settlement of the estate. The law requires the bond for their protection, and the parties interested acquire a vested interest in the bond which cannot be divested without their consent, except in the manner prescribed by the statute. Unless empowered to do so by the statute, the court is without authority to discharge or release a surety or bonding company, except with the consent of the parties interested.

The statutes of some states require even the child's natural guardian to put up a bond before gaining control over the estate of the child. (Alabama, Georgia, Maryland, Missouri, Montana, New Jersey.) Some statutes give the judge discretion to waive the posting of a bond by the guardian under all or special circumstances depending upon the language of the particular statute involved. It is self-evident that the requirements of the particular statute as to the form and sufficiency of the bond must be conformed to, and it is especially important that the bond should run in favor of the person named in the statute as otherwise it may be void. The bond may be payable to a ward named therein, to the surrogate, the county judge, a justice of the peace or the state itself, varying with the requirements of the various statutes.

E. LIABILITY UNDER THE BOND

The bond is a continuing obligation which will run until the guardian and the sureties are discharged, which happens, usually after the final account has been judicially settled. The bond will be for a certain specified amount as a penalty for non-performance of the guardian's obligations under the statute; some states require sureties to execute the bond along with the principal obligor. It is the general rule that unless the particular statute specifically authorizes the reduction of the amount of the penalty specified in the bond, the court is powerless to reduce the amount although in at least one state it has been held that the trial court has implied power to reduce the amount of the bond. It is permissible for one bond to be posted for the benefit of more than one ward. Under such a joint bond the aggregate liability cannot exceed the amount of the penalty specified in the bond, with interest, from the time demand is made. Also in an action by a ward against the surety or bonding company on a guardian's bond running to several wards jointly, the other wards are not necessary parties to the action. It is the purpose of the bond to protect the individual rights of each ward and where the determination of the controversy with one ward will not prejudice the other wards the court may therefore determine the issues raised without their presence. However, when a complete determination of the controversy cannot be had without the presence of other parties the court may order them to be brought in.

If the guardian does not perform faithfully and in accordance with the statutory requirements all duties required of him then the surety or bonding company becomes liable on the bond. While the surety is liable for the guardian's failure to perform the general duties imposed upon him by law, as such guardian, the surety is not liable for the guardian's failure to perform any special and additional duty imposed upon him which does not come within the scope of the general guardianship.

F. SPECIAL SALE BOND

A guardian, contemplating a specific sale of real property

belonging to his infant ward, may be required to file what is known as a special sale bond to cover the specific transaction. In such cases, the surety on the general bond of a guardian is not liable for any neglect or defalcation of the guardian in connection with his duties arising out of the real estate transaction.

G. SURETY'S LIABILITY

The guardian must act in good faith, and must exercise ordinary intelligence, care and prudence in connection with the performance of his guardianship duties. Where the guardian is guilty of negligence or bad faith in the performance of his obligations then both he and the surety will be held liable for the resultant damage to the ward's property. For example, where a guardian without authority from the probate court, deposited the ward's money in a savings account and the guardian was later informed that the bank in which the deposit was made was of doubtful solvency but the guardian in spite of this knowledge neglected to withdraw the money, and instead obtained a court order authorizing the deposit, and later the bank became insolvent, the court held both the guardian and the bonding company liable for the amount of the funds deposited in the bank. Likewise, it has been held that where a bank acting as guardian neglects to invest its ward's money but instead places the money with the bank's general funds and the bank subsequently becomes insolvent the surety is liable for the amount lost by the ward. Knowledge on the part of the bonding company of the guardian's default or neglect in the performance of his duties is not necessary; it will be held liable regardless, for any breach of the guardian's obligation.

It must not be presumed, however, that just because a bank in which the guardian deposits the ward's money fails that the guardian will be liable; there must be an act of bad faith or neglect amounting to a breach of the guardian's duties such as making a deposit without authorization, in order for liability for loss to follow. The guardian and surety will, of course, be held liable for any improper or unauthorized loans or investments made in violation of the statute. The court's approval must be first had and obtained for any investment made by the guardian of the ward's money in securities not specifically authorized by the governing statute.

It is the general rule that the guardian must pay for the maintenance and education of the ward out of the property under the guardian's control. Failure to do this constitutes a breach of the guardian's general bond and the bonding company would be liable for such breach.

Likewise it is the duty of the guardian to pay all debts of the ward, having due regard to priorities which may exist among creditors. Such payment must be made in full if the property is sufficient for that purpose; if insufficient, then pro rata.

Upon the conclusion of the guardianship or at the time specified by law it becomes the duty of the guardian to account for and settle the affairs of the guardianship. Failure to do this amounts to a breach of the guardian's bond for which the bonding company can be held liable. It is the general rule that the surety cannot be held liable for misfeasance by the guardian prior in time to the execution of the bond signed by the surety. However, two states take the view that the surety is liable for the guardian's defaults occurring before the execution of the surety bond. (Nebraska, Oklahoma.) Such courts take the view that it is immaterial when the conversion or misappropriation took place, or from what source the funds in the hands of the guardian were derived. Under this minority rule when the settlement of the guardian's transaction is effected, and the order of the court made, directing him to turn over a specified amount, there is nothing left for the guardian to do but pay over the amount or appeal from the order; and if such judgment and order becomes final and are not obeyed by the guardian, a breach of the bond is effected and the surety is liable for the default. Some states take the view that the surety is liable for conversion of funds prior to the execution of the bond if the guardian was in fact solvent at the time the bond was given. (Mississippi, Missouri, Texas and Washington.)

Where a second or cumulative bond is given it is generally held that such bond covers all past defaults and misconduct by the guardian and the surety on such second bond will be liable for all past improper acts of the guardian. Some state statutes require renewal bonds and these are interpreted as being cumulative and the bonding company's liability extends back to the date of the guardian's appointment.

As we have mentioned previously, the surety on a guardian's special bond for the sale of real estate executed in compliance with the particular statutory requirement is not liable for misappropriation by the guardian of funds not arising from the sale of real estate. Where the statute requires a bond to cover the proceeds of the sale of real estate in addition to the general bond of the guardian then it covers only the collection and disposition of the purchase price of the real property. If the guardian fails to collect, or after collecting fails to turn over or properly account for the purchase price as required of him then liability accrues to the surety on the special bond.

In those states where the general bond as well as the special sale bond is interpreted to cover the sale of the ward's real estate then the special bond is generally regarded as cumulative, and the sureties on both bonds will be liable for the guardian's misappropriation.

H. CONDITIONS TERMINATING GUARDIANSHIP

The guardian's appointment continues during the minority of the child unless the order of appointment limits the term of his office. Naturally, the death, resignation as incapacitation of the guardian will automatically terminate the office of the guardian. When an individual person rather than a corporation or bonding company is the surety on the guardian's bond, the death of such surety obligates the court to appoint a new surety. If the ward dies during the term of the guardianship, the guardian is required forthwith to make the necessary accounting in compliance with the statute. Where the guardian has several wards under his supervision and care, the death of one merely terminates the guardianship as to the deceased and does not affect the surviving wards.

The attainment of the ward's majority usually terminates the guardianship. The reason for this rule of law is that upon reaching such age limit the ward is entitled to demand that the guardian account and settle.

Since the death of either the guardian or the ward ends the guardianship, it also starts the running of the statute of limitations in favor of the guardian and the surety on the guardian's bond. Likewise the attainment by the ward of his majority constitutes termination of the guardianship for the purpose of putting into operation the statute of limitations in favor of the guardian and the surety on the bond.

Naturally after a ward attains his majority the guardian is no longer entitled to represent him in pending litigation. But as a suit commenced by the guardian during the ward's minority is actually the suit of the ward, it does not end in the event of the guardian's death during the litigation. The deceased guardian is merely eliminated from the case and the suit continues with the minor being represented either by a new general guardian or special guardian for the purpose of the law suit, a *guardian ad litem*.

Some state statutes provide, in effect, that the guardian is charged with the care and management of the ward's estate until the minor attains majority or marries. Such statutes are not intended to prolong the guardian's control of either the person or the estate of the minor beyond the date when such ward shall attain the age of majority, and the guardian's authority, of course, ceases at that point. In some states the marriage of the ward during minority causes the authority of the guardian to cease as to the ward's person only, but not as to the estate; in other states the marriage of the ward terminates the guardianship only where the ward is a female.

Where the guardian is an unmarried female her marriage does not terminate the guardianship but generally imposes upon her husband the obligation of jointly carrying out the guardianship.

I. ALLOWANCES OR COMPENSATION TO GUARDIAN

Generally a guardian is allowed the same commissions on income or revenue as an executor, trustee or administrator. Usually a court will make allowances for any special service rendered by the guardian and will allow to the guardian reasonable expenses and attorney's fees. A few states have special commission rates for guardians. (See chart in Appendix.)

J. FOREIGN GUARDIANS

It sometimes happens that an infant or an incompetent person owns property in a state other than the one in which he resides. Obviously, someone in that other state must be empowered to act for him. A similar situation also arises where a deceased parent names a non-resident as a testamentary guardian for his surviving child. It is important, in such cases to know whether the courts of the child's residence can, or may, permit a non-resident to act for the child, within the state. It is also important to know whether the guardian appointed in one state has the right to act in another where the child may have property. All states have laws relating to the selection and control of guardians of this type.

The common law rule is that a foreign guardian has no rights, powers or functions except where appointed.

In many states, a guardian appointed in the state of residence may act within the other state without formal appointment as guardian in the second state. (However, many states prohibit a foreign corporation or trust company from acting within their state limits, as a guardian of the estate of an infant ward or incompetent person.) Furthermore, many states permit a foreign, guardian (i.e., one appointed in another state) to remove assets of a non-resident ward simply upon a showing of his appointment as such guardian.

Some states require that before a guardian appointed in another state may act within its territorial limits, he must be appointed by its courts and be subject to its limitations. Some states restrict further the rights of the guardian appointed in another state. Some require that he be a resident of the state where he is now seeking to act, or entirely prohibit him from acting unless he can qualify within the state as a guardian. In such cases, it will be necessary to appoint a local guardian.

As indicated above, the guardian who acts in a state other that that of his appointment is generally known as a *foreign guardian.* A guardian who is appointed by a state other than that in which guardianship was originally granted (that is, where there is already a guardian acting in another state) is called the *ancillary guardian.*

In general, the foreign guardian has no powers except in the state of his appointment; his powers in any other place depend on the laws of that other place, either as they appear in the statutes or as the courts have decided. He may be empowered to act in another jurisdiction in one of two ways. First, he may qualify as a guardian under the laws of that second state. He must meet, in this case, all the formalities and statutory requirements affecting local guardians. In other words, it is really a new appointment and his appointment in one state does relieve him of the duty of complying with the second state's requirements. Second, a foreign guardian may by the laws of the second state be recognized as a guardian and be granted certain rights over the property of the ward, within limits, without being formally appointed by the local courts but simply upon proof of his appointment in another state and the residence of his ward.

Some states will permit a foreign guardian to remove personal property of a ward or proceeds from the sale of real property to the state of domicile. The court may even permit the guardian to remove a ward to another state. He may be permitted to remove property or proceeds either directly or through the appointment of a local guardian, or ancillary guardian.

K. ANCILLARY GUARDIAN

In certain cases (for example, where the ward has property within the state) the court may appoint a local guard-

63

ian to act in local matters where original guardian was appointed out of the state. Preference may, and generally is, given to the originally appointed guardian, subject to requirements of the statutes. Even where statutes permit appointment of the foreign guardian for the state, the matter still rests in the discretion of the courts and the most important factor at all times is the welfare of the ward.

Ancillary letters give powers only as to specific estate or the property mentioned and are not in any sense a general appointment.

In general, foreign guardians even when permitted to act within the state, may not sue within the state.

Chapter 4

GUARDIANS OF OTHER INCOMPETENTS

In discussing guardianships over this special class of persons it should be remembered that the incompetency of an alcoholic or spendthrift, which requires that a guardian be appointed, is not the same type of incompetency which exists in one declared insane. In the latter situation it is necessary for the mental incompetent to have a guardian appointed to look after his business affairs because of a lack of mental capacity while in the case of the alcoholic or spendthrift it is generally not lack of intelligence but an inability of character making the individual totally irresponsible. There is a presumption of sanity which must be overcome in cases where it is attempted to prove a person incompetent because of unsound mind. No presumption exists in cases of alcoholics and spendthrifts.

A. INSANE PERSONS. INQUISITION

Before a guardian can be appointed for any alleged incompetent it is necessary that a finding be made by a court of competent jurisdiction that the individual is incompetent to manage his affairs. It is necessary that sufficient evidence support a finding that a person is an incompetent and that, therefore, a guardian should be appointed to handle his affairs. The proceeding is generally known as an "inquisition", and the guardian of an incompetent person, more generally known as the "committee" or "conservator".

The appointment of a guardian for an incompetent person is in most states strictly regulated by statutes, most of which provide that any person having the interest of the

65

alleged incompetent in mind is sufficiently qualified for appointment as guardian. The appointment of a relative or friend as guardian is intended by the statutes to guarantee that a person favorably disposed toward the incompetent will act for his interest and benefit. The courts will not adjudge a mere busybody, a stranger or an ex-wife to be a friend within the meaning given to the word by the statutes. (In fact, some states even exclude present spouses; however, spouses and close relatives are generally preferred.) The word "friend," has been given a broad and varied application and no particular degree of intimacy is required in order that a person commencing an action to adjudicate the competency of another individual be considered a friend of the alleged incompetent person. The proceedings for the appointment of a guardian may in fact be commenced by a relative, a friend or the incompetent himself. The proceedings must comply strictly with the statutory requirements and if a committee or commission is required by the particular statute then the hearing and findings of such commission must be in conformance with the law.

B. Duties of Guardian

The guardian or committee appointed to look after the affairs of an incompetent is in the same fiduciary relationship to the incompetent as the general guardian is to the minor ward and is in general subject to the same rules with respect to accountings, obligations to provide support and necessaries out of the incompetent's estate, business dealings and investments, sale and management of real property, fees and compensation for the guardian or committee and removal of the guardian or committee. The actual care of a lunatic is usually not a problem for the guardian or committee as the insane person is almost always placed in an institution. In the cases of drunkards and idiots also, under some statutes, authority exists to place the incompetent in an institution. Where statutory authorization does not exist, the courts will pretty generally follow the guardian's or committee's recommendations as to confinement of an incompetent.

In Louisiana the same rule applies to the appointment of a guardian or committee for a mental incompetent as in the case of appointment of a general guardian for a minor ward—it is necessary in that state for the request for a guardian to come to the court as a result of a family meeting except in the case of husband and wife.

In incompetency proceedings it is not at all unusual for a temporary guardian to be appointed by the court where the welfare of the individual requires it to be done.

Unless provided for by the particular statute no appeal may be taken, as of right, from an order or decree appointing a guardian for one who has been adjudicated an incompetent. The result of a decision to the effect that an individual is incompetent, is to make such person, a ward of the court and to give control over such property as the incompetent may possess to the guardian appointed by the court on his behalf. As we have noted above in connection with the appointment of guardians for the property of minor wards, a properly qualified corporation may administer the property of an incompetent where authorized by the particular statute.

C. TERMINATION OF INCOMPETENT'S COMMITTEE

The death of either the guardian or the incompetent terminates the guardianship; the guardianship is also ended by the incompetent being later adjudged competent.

The requirements governing the posting of a bond by the guardian of an incompetent are by statute generally the same as we have seen in Chapter Six, above, and likewise the provisions with respect to sureties are usually identical.

In the case of an incompetent who has been adjudicated such because of insanity, the statutes generally provide for such a person's release upon his regaining a sound mental condition. Where the statutes are silent on this point, the release of the patient generally rests in the discretion of the officials of the institution of confinement or the court. Upon release, the incompetent can petition the court for the discharge of the guardian or committee, and upon such petition being presented in proper form the court will conduct a hearing to decide the question of discharge of the committee and restoration of the incompetent's affairs to his own hands. Some statutes provide for a waiting period after release from the institution before a guardian or committee can be discharged.

Most statutes provide that the alleged incompetent is entitled to be present at the hearing on the question of his competency; many statutes now provide that a doctor's certificate of insanity is necessary as part of the proof before any person can be adjudged insane or committed. Where a statute so provides for the certificate or testimony of one or more physicians then such proof must be produced in strict compliance with the statute, because the outcome of the proceedings affects the right of the individual to the enjoyment of life, liberty and property; and in some states the legislature has even gone so far as to authorize the sterilization of insane or feeble-minded persons.

Because of the presence of the element of confinement of the insane in institutions, the statutes in some states distinguish between the general guardian of an infant ward and the guardian of an incompetent person in that the guardian of an incompetent has only power over the property of the incompetent; and this applies to all types of incompetents, whereas we have seen that the general guardian of an infant ward has custody of the person and property of such ward. Likewise these same statutes provide that the committee of the person of the incompetent is without authority over the incompetent's property. In other jurisdictions the power and authority of the guardian and the committee are co-extensive. Most statutes provide that the title to the incompetent's estate remains in the name of the incompetent, while the guardian or committee has possession, control and management of the property until such time as the court shall order otherwise.

The rules outlined above apply as well to incompetent veterans except where the Uniform Veterans' Guardianship Act has been adopted. (See next chapter) Where it has been enacted its provisions are controlling, if in conflict with the general rules and strict compliance with its terms is required.

In most states an incompetent has the right to sue or be sued, and in the event of litigation a guardian *ad litem* will be appointed to represent the incompetent. The guardian or committee of the incompetent is under a duty to see that the incompetent's legal interests are protected and to sue to enforce any claims which the incompetent may have.

D. SPENDTHRIFTS

Before concluding, a few words should be said in connection with spendthrifts—a spendthrift has been defined by a Maine statute as one "who spends or wastes his estate so as to expose himself or his family to want or suffering or his town to expense." A spendthrift then is a heedless, improvident, wasteful person who needs the protection of a guardian in the management of his property.

Generally, any person who is an inhabitant of the community in which the spendthrift himself resides, including the spendthrift himself, can institute a proceeding for the appointment of a guardian for the alleged spendthrift. The requirements of the statute must be strictly complied with, and the procedure is generally the same as we have already seen in guardianship cases with the proceeding started by petition, a hearing and determination by the court, the appointment of the guardian upon an affirmative finding, and appeal from the court decision only if permitted by statute. The usual rules as to the liability of the guardian and sureties on the bond prevail in spendthrift cases.

Chapter 5

VETERAN'S GUARDIANSHIP

A. SPECIAL LEGISLATION CONTROLS

In the absence of any special legislation, the affairs of veteran incompetents, minors or their beneficiaries who suffer from incapacity requiring guardianship are controlled by the laws of the state in which they reside. In the majority of the states, however, special provisions have been made for the handling of affairs of veterans or their beneficiaries who require guardianship of one sort or another. In such cases, of course, the appointment of guardians, limitations upon investments, compensation of guardians and all other aspects of the matter are subject to the special legislation.

B. HISTORY OF UNIFORM LAW

Because of the diversity of benefits, and of beneficiaries, and the great number of them, and the fact that assets of the veteran come mainly from one source—The Veteran's Administration—a uniform law was proposed which would apply in all states adopting such law. This was called the Uniform Veterans Guardianship Act. The first such act was proposed in 1928 and was almost immediately adopted

Veterans and their dependents are entitled to various benefits, generally derived from the United States Government and arising out of the status of veteran. The benefits may differ depending on the type and length of service, and the relationship of the veteran to his beneficiary. There may be children or wives. The veteran himself may be a minor. Some beneficiaries may be incompetent. Furthermore, the beneficiaries may be spread throughout the United States. Since the benefits are administered to a great extent by the Veterans Administration (which is always a party in interest in any proceeding affecting the veteran or his beneficiaries) through the courts of the United States, and each matter requires the approval and guidance of those courts, it can readily be seen that uniformity among the laws of the various states is greatly to be desired.

The original 1928 Act was followed by the 1942 Uniform Veterans Guardianship Act, which put into effect a number of desired and recommended changes. With few exceptions, it is the law in effect today in all those states which have adopted it. Chart 3 which follows this Chapter indicates, among other things, adopting states.

C. APPOINTMENT OF GUARDIAN

As indicated above, this law makes the Administrator of Veterans Affairs a party in interest in any proceeding affecting an incompetent or minor veteran or beneficiary of the United States. The provisions of this act are mandatory as to any funds derived from the Veterans Administration of the United States by a veteran ward or his beneficiaries who are wards. A guardian may, however, include in his accounting funds received from sources other than the Veterans Administration. A guardian under this law may not have more than five wards under his guardianship, unless they are all in the same family.

Again the status of the person for whom the guardian is sought to be appointed must be shown. For an infant, proof of age is relatively simple today. Mental incompetency of the beneficiary must be adjudicated by the court. The certificate of the Veterans Administrator to the effect that a beneficiary is under age or has been rated incompetent is generally enough, in the absence of other proof to the contrary to show that status of the person for whom the guardian is being appointed. The ward is given notice of the proceedings to determine his competency or status. If a guardian is appointed, a bond is required, to be filed as in non-veteran guardianships, to insure the faithful performance of the guardian's duties.

D. GUARDIAN'S ACCOUNTS

Under the uniform law, the guardian must file an account annually upon the anniversary of his appointment, together with receipts showing disbursements and certified statements of deposits and investments of the ward. An alternate provision of this law permits filing of accounts at three years intervals. Individual state laws should be consulted to determine which of these alternatives is applicable.

Most states require annual filing. However, even in those states where state laws require court filing only once in three years, an annual account must still be filed in the office of the Veterans Administration.

E. Guardian's Compensation

The uniform law provides that the compensation of a veteran guardian shall not exceed 5% of the amounts received during the period for which he is accounting, unless special circumstances requiring unusual and additional services to be rendered by the guardian are proved to the satisfaction of the court.

F. Guardian's Duty to Invest

Surplus funds of the ward are required to be invested by the guardian. He cannot put the money in a non-interest bearing account and keep it unproductive though safe. There are severe limitations upon the securities in which investment may be made so that the guardian does not have the right to speculate with his ward's funds.

G. Discharge of Guardian and Release of Surety

In addition to the usual requirements, there must also be attached to an application for discharge and release of a guardian and surety, a certificate from the Veterans Administration showing that the disability under which the ward suffered no longer exists. The court will not discharge and release the guardian and his surety in the absence of such a certificate.

H. Guardian's Duties and Responsibilities

Basically, the duties and responsibilities of a veteran's guardian are the same as those of other guardians. The chief point of difference is that, at all stages of the proceedings, the Veterans Administrator is a party in interest and, as such vitally concerned with the management and condition of the ward's affairs. It must be kept advised of the status of the ward's affairs at all times. In its efforts to gain uniformity and to facilitate its job of administering veterans matters, the Veterans Administration has prepared and will supply forms and instructions covering all aspects of a guardian's management of the ward's property and other affairs.

I. Relationship of the Uniform to State Laws

It must be remembered that the Uniform law applies only in the states which have adopted it. The states may adopt only portions of it controlling procedure in certain respects and retain its customary practice in other respects. The extent of the adoption of the uniform law can be determined by examining the state laws.

Chart 3
DIGEST OF STATE LAWS DEALING
WITH VETERAN GUARDIANSHIPS

State	Resume	Citation
ALABAMA	Uniform Veterans' Guardianship Act with modifications. Provides for the appointment of a guardian of an incompetent veteran or minor child of a veteran, to receive certain benefits on behalf of such ward.	Title 21, ## 160-176.
ALASKA	*Estates* The Administrator of Veterans' Affairs is to be made a party in interest and to be furnished with copies of accountings when an estate to be administered by a guardian includes assets derived from benefits paid by the Veterans' Administration.	#20.05.170, 190.
ARIZONA	Generally - protection of property of persons under disability and minors.	#14-5401-54 32.
	Appointment of conservators of estates of persons detained by a foreign power or who have disappeared.	#14-5401.
	Annual accounting of conservator to Veterans' Administration.	#14-5421.
	Accountings - copy to Veterans' Administration..........	#14-5419B.

State	Resume	Citation

Bond - provided at request of VA................ #14-5411B.

Bond - "interested person" may bring action on bond of conservator............... #14-5412.

Incapacity - certificate by Veterans' Administration as prima facie evidence............... #14-5406.

Interested person - includes Governmental agency.......... #5407C.

Inventory and records - exhibited to any "interested person" #14-5418.

Notice - notice of petition for appointment of conservator to "interested persons." #14-5405

-Department of Security, compensation when acting as guardian shall be 3 percent of the amount of moneys received during the period covered by the guardianship. Court may authorize reasonable additional compensation in event of extraordinary service. #14-892B.

ARKANSAS   *Appointment of guardians for incompetent veterans.* - Provisions cumulative to Uniform Guardianship Act.   1971 replacement, ##57-601 to 57-647.

Uniform Guardianship Act. - Provides for the appointment of a guardian of an incompetent   1971 replacement, ##57-501

State	Resume	Citation
	veteran or minor child of a veteran, to receive certain benefits on behalf of such ward.	57-522.
CALIFORNIA	Uniform Veterans Guardianship Act with modifications. Provides for appointment of guardian of incompetent or minor entitled to receive benefits from Veterans Administration, and requires notice of certain steps in the proceeding to Veterans' Administration.	Probate Code #1650-1669.
	-Conservator may be appointed instead of a guardian..........	Probate Code, #2151
	Veterans Home of California.- May be appointed Guardian of the estate of a member veteran.	Military & Veterans Code ## 1046, 1035-1039.
	-Personal property held by Home at death of member veteran vests in Home's Post Fund with certain limited exceptions.	
COLORADO	*Uniform Veterans' Guardianship Act.* - Provides for appointment of a guardian of an incompetent veteran of minor child of a veteran to receive certain benefits on behalf of such ward.	C.R.S. (1963) 144-3-1 to 144-3-23.
CONNECTI-CUT	Administration of veterans' estates by the Veterans' Home and Hospital Commission under certain	Gen.Stat. (1958), ## 27-118, 45-58.

State	Resume	Citation

circumstances; Administrator of Veterans' Affairs to be made party in interest.

Appointment of conservator for incompetent veteran contingent upon certificate from Veterans' Administration that such person is rated incompetent and appointment is condition to receiving money due.

Gen.Stat. (1958), #27-129.

Guardian, appointment of. -Administrator of Veterans' Affairs shall be made a party in interest in proceedings for appointment of a guardian.

Gen.Stat. (1958), # 45-58.

Guardian of a veteran, compensation of..........

Gen.Stat. (1958), # 45-60.

DELAWARE Trustee of guardian may be appointed to receive, on behalf of a veteran or other person, moneys payable by the U.S. Government.

Code Ann. (1953), 12-3508.

FLORIDA *Guardians of Incompetent veterans.* -Provisions of the Florida guardianship law shall apply to: Florida deeds executed by guardians appointed under guardianship law, validity.

#744-05.

#694.14(1).

Guardians may be appointed under supplement veterans' guardianship law for persons entitled to benefits under the War Risk Insurance Act and World War Veterans' Act of 1924.

##294.01 to 294.12.

State	Resume	Citation
	Uniform Veterans' Guardianship Act. -Provides for the appointment of a guardian of an incompetent veteran or the minor child of a veteran, to receive certain benefits on behalf of such ward.	##293.01 to 293.20.
GEORGIA	*Uniform Veterans' Guardianship Act* with modifications. -Provides for appointment of a guardian of an incompetent veteran or the minor child of a veteran, to receive benefits on behalf of such ward.	Code Ann., (1936 ed.), ## 49-801 to 49-818.
HAWAII	*Uniform Veterans' Guardianship Act.* -Provides for the appointment of a guardian of an incompetent veteran or the minor child of a veteran, to receive benefits on behalf of such ward.	#552-1 to 552-19
IDAHO	Notice to the Veterans' Administration or other agency, bureau or department of the United States of certain proceedings under the law on guardian and ward.	Idaho Code No. 15-5-405 and No. 15-5-406.
	Uniform Probate Code. -Provides for appointment of a guardian of an incompetent veteran or the minor child of a veteran to receive certain benefits on behalf of such ward.	Idaho Code No. 15-5-301 to No. 15-5-313.
ILLINOIS	Limits the interest of the Administrator of Veterans' Affairs	Rev.Stat. 3, ## 9a., 122 and 140.

in the estate of a minor or incompetent to that part of the estate derived from payments made directly to the estate by the Veterans' Administration. Requires guardians and conservators making application for leave to invest ward's funds or expend such funds for the support or education of any person entitled thereto, to give notice to the chief attorney of the administrator of Veterans' Affairs, in the State.

No costs shall be taxed or charged by any public officer in cases involving the appointment of a guardian, or the collection, disbursement, or administering of moneys awarded by the Veterans' Administration to the ward, or in proceedings to obtain benefits pursuant to the Servicemen's Readjustment Act.

Rev.Stat. 3, #146a.

Conservators. -Appointments for mentally incompetent beneficiaries of the Veterans' Administration; no costs to be charged except court, in its discretion, may allow costs where there are no assets not derived from the Veterans' Administration.

Rev.Stat. 3, #118a.

-Notice of hearing on revocation of conservatorship....

Rev.Stat. 3, #130.

Waiver of bond of guardian of Veterans' estates in certain cases; accounts.

Rev.Stat. 3, ## 152, 310.

State	Resume	Citation
	No fees are allowed public administrators for service performed in administering that part of the personal estate of a war veteran which consists of compensation, insurance, or other moneys due or payable from the United States.	Rev.Stat. 3, #336.
INDIANA	Uniform Veterans' Guardianship Act with modifications. Provides for the appointment of a guardian of an incompetent veteran or the minor child of a veteran, to receive certain benefits on behalf of such ward.	IC 29-1-19 et seq. (Burns 8-201 et seq.).
IOWA	*Uniform Veterans' Guardianship or Conservator Act* with modifications. -Provides for the appointment of a guardian or conservator of an incompetent veteran, or the minor child of a veteran, to receive certain benefits on behalf of such ward.	Code 1973), ##663.614 to 663.622.
KANSAS	None	
KENTUCKY	*Uniform Veterans' Guardianship Act* with modifications. -Provides for appointment of a guardian of an incompetent veteran or the minor child of a veteran, to receive certain benefits on behalf of such ward.	K.R.S., ## 388.190 to 388.390.
	Uniform Veterans' Guardianship Act. - K.R.S. #388.300 was amended, effective June 14, 1962, to provide for a minimum compen-	K.R.S. (1963), ## 338.190 to

State	Resume	Citation
	sation fee of $50 per year due all fiduciaries of VA beneficiaries.	388.390.
LOUISIANA	*Union Veterans' Guardianship Act.* -Provides for appointment of a guardian of an incompetent veteran or the minor child of a veteran to receive certain benefits on behalf of such ward. Age of majority reduced from 21 to 18 years of age..........	Rev.Stat. 29:351-372, and 1966 Cum. Pockets Parts. Act. 98 of 1972.
MAINE	*Uniform Veterans' Guardianship Act.* -Provides for the appointment of a guardian of an incompetent veteran or the minor child of a veteran.	Title 37, MRSA, ## 201-221.
MARYLAND	*Veterans' Guardianship.* -Provides for the appointment of a guardian of an incompetent veteran or the minor child of a veteran, to receive certain benefits on behalf of such ward.	Art. 93A,## 801-806.
MASSACHU-SETTS	Notice shall be given to the Veterans' Administration of an accounting by a guardian if the award is entitled to any benefit, estate, or income payable through the Administration.	Ch. 206, #7.
	Notice shall be given to the Veterans' Administration of the appointment of a guardian or conservator for an adult or minor beneficiary of such agency.	Ch. 201, ## 2,7, and 17.
	The Veterans' Administration may act as guardian ad litem in certain cases.	Ch. 206, # 24.

State	Resume	Citation
MICHIGAN	The commandment of the Michigan Soldiers' Home (now State Veterans' Facility), may be appointed guardian of a member of the home in certain cases.	1969 Rev. vol., ## 4.931 to 4.935.
	Uniform Veterans' Guardianship Act with modifications. Provides for the appointment of a guardian of an incompetent veteran or the minor child of a veteran, to receive certain benefits on behalf of such ward.	1969 Rev. vol., ## 4.971(1) to 4.971(21).
MINNESOTA	Notice of a hearing on account of a guardian to be given the regional office of the Veterans' Administration.	#525.581.
	The commissioner of veterans' affairs shall act as guardian for a minor or incompetent person receiving moneys from the U.S. Government when requested to do so by an agency of the United States of America provided sufficient personnel are available to do so.	1971 Cum. Pocket Part, ## 196.5(11), law, amended by laws 1963 Ch. 132, #1.
MISSISSIPPI	Uniform Veterans' Guardianship Act, with modifications. Provides for the appointment of a guardian of an incompetent veteran, or the minor child of a veteran, to receive certain benefits on behalf of such ward.	35-5-3 to 35-5-33.

State	Resume	Citation
MISSOURI	*Uniform Veterans' Guardianship Law,* with modifications. Provides for appointment of a guardian of an incompetent veteran, or the minor child of a veteran to receive certain benefits on behalf of such ward.	V.A.M.S., #475.380 to 475.480.
MONTANA	*Uniform Guardianship Act.* -Provides for the appointment of a guardian of an incompetent veteran or his minor child, to receive certain benefits of such ward.	Rev.Codes, 1947, ## 91-4801 to 91-4822
NEBRASKA	*Uniform Veterans' Guardianship.* -Provides for the appointment of a guardian of an incompetent veteran or the minor child of a veteran, to receive certain benefits on behalf of such ward.	R.R.S. 1943 #38-401 to 38-421.
	Authorizes district courts to appoint *conservators* over property owned either singly or jointly by prisoners of war or persons missing in action.	R.R.S. 1943, #25-21, 168 to 25-21, 179.
NEVADA	Uniform Veterans' Guardianship providing for protection through judicially appointed fiduciaries of Veterans' Administration beneficiaries under legal disability.	N.R.S., ch. 160.
	Conservators. -provides for conservators for protection estates of persons missing in action.	

State	Resume	Citation
NEW HAMPSHIRE	Uniform Veterans' Guardianship Act. with modifications. Provides for the appointment of a guardian of an incompetent veteran or the minor child of a veteran, to receive certain benefits on behalf of such ward.	R.S.A., # 465: 1-14.
	State veterans' council director is exempt from certain limitations of law when acting as guardian.	R.S.A., # 465: 3, 5, 11.
NEW JERSEY	County public guardian of incompetent veterans to assist guardians of incompetent veterans.	##3A:31-1 to 31-11.
	Parent of minor may administer estates of less than $3,000 combined value of realty and personally without appointment as guardian.	##3A:6-31 to 6-32.
	Receipt, investment, etc., by guardian of personal property valued at less than $2,500, to which the ward shall become entitled from any source other than the Federal Government, is regulated.	##3A: 30-4 to 30-6.
	Uniform Veterans' Guardianship Act with modifications. -Provides for the appointment of a guardian of an incompetent veteran or the minor child of a veteran to receive certain benefits on behalf of such ward.	##3A:27-1 to 31-11.

State	Resume	Citation
NEW MEXICO	The Veterans' Service Commission may act as administrator or executor of the estate of a deceased veteran or as the guardian of an incompetent veteran or of a minor child of a veteran; or as a guardian of any resident of the State having money due from Veterans' Administration, payment of which is dependent upon appointment of guardian.	##74-1-9 to 74-1-11.
NEW YORK	*Uniform Veterans' Guardianship Act* with modifications. -Provides for the appointment of a guardian of an incompetent veteran or the minor child of a veteran, to receive certain benefits on behalf of such ward.	Mental Hygiene Law, art. 79. ch. 251, Laws of 1971.
	World War II bonus payments to a minor or mental incompetent..........	Unconsolidated Laws, #9701.
NORTH CAROLINA	Clerk of the superior court to act as temporary guardian and to receive and disburse allotments to children of servicemen.	Gen.Stats. # 33-67.
	Uniform Guardianship Act with modifications. Provides for the appointment of a guardian of an incompetent veteran or the minor child of a veteran, to receive certain benefits. Provides for procedure accounting, supervision, and management of wards' estates.	Gen.Stats. 1971 Supp. (Session Laws 1973) ##34-1 to 34-18.

State	Resume	Citation
OHIO	No probate court costs shall be taxed in proceedings involving the collection, disbursement, or administering of money awarded by the Veterans' Administration.	#2111.02.
	The Superintendent of the Ohio Soldiers' and Sailors' Home shall be guardian of the estate of all minors admitted to the home.	#5909.04.
	Uniform Veterans' Guardianship Act. -Provides for the appointment of a guardian of an incompetent veteran or the minor child of a veteran, to receive certain benefits on behalf of such ward.	##5905.02-5909.19.
OKLAHOMA	Court costs shall not be required in any proceeding to appoint a guardian to approve or authorize the ward to enter the Armed Forces.	Title 58, # 782.
	Uniform Veterans' Guardianship Act and revised Act. Provides for appointment of a guardian of an incompetent veteran or the minor child of a veteran, to receive certain benefits on behalf of such ward.	Title 72, ## 126.1-126.23.
	Minors defined as persons, male and female, under the age of 18 years.	title 15, #13.

State	Resume	Citation
OREGON	Notice may be served by Veterans Administration upon conservator of estate of veteran, requesting that a copy of all accounts, petitions for sale, lease or mortgage of property or investment of funds of estate, be served upon a representative of the Veterans' Administration.	Ch. 823. Oregon Laws 1973.
	The Director of Veterans' Affairs of Oregon shall have authority to act without bond as conservator of the estate of a Veterans' Administration beneficiary who is an incompetent, spendthrift or minor, when he determines no other suitable person will so act.	ORS. ## 408.010-408.090.
PENNSYL-VANIA	Provides for notice to the U.S. Veterans Administration of proceedings for the appointment of a guardian of a veteran of a minor child or incompetent dependent of veteran on whose account benefits of compensation of insurance or other gratuity is payable. Makes the Veterans' Administration a party in interest on the filing of an account by the guardian.	20 P.S., ## 788, 789.
RHODE ISLAND	Exemption from payment of probate fees where the appointment of a guardian is for the purpose of receiving benefits of laws administered by the U.S. Veterans' Administration.	#33-22-22.

State	Resume	Citation
	Uniform Veterans' Guardianship Act. Provides for the appointment of a guardian of an incompetent veteran or the minor child of a veteran, to receive certain benefits on behalf of such ward.	#33-16-1 to 33-16-35.
SOUTH CAROLINA	*Uniform Veterans' Guardianship Act.* Appointment, fitness, and duties of guardian (committee) of veterans or minors to receive benefits for such ward.	#31-201 to 31-227.
SOUTH DAKOTA	Provision is made for appointment of a guardian for persons entitled to benefits under war-risk insurance and World War veterans' acts.	#30-33-9.
	Uniform Veterans' Guardianship Act. Provision is made for the appointment of a guardian or an incompetent veteran or the minor child of a veteran, to receive certain benefits on behalf of such ward.	##30-33-1 to 30-33-47.
TENNESSEE	Provisions for appointment of conservator of estates of absentees serving with Armed Forces in period of hostilities, and for 1 year thereafter, who have been reported or listed as missing in action, interned in a neutral country, beleaguered, besieged, or captured by the enemy.	##30-1901 to 30-1911.

State	Resume	Citation
	Uniform veterans' guardianship law provides for the appointment of a guardian of an incompetent veteran or his minor child, to receive certain benefits on behalf of such ward.	##34-901 to 34-922.
TEXAS	Appointment of a guardian of a minor, imcompetent, or other person, when necessary to receive funds from any governmental source or agency.	Probate Court. #4.
	Purchase by guardian of life insurance policies administered by the Veterans' Administration.	Probate Code, #390.
	Provides for notice to Veterans' Administration of the filing of accounts and of certain other proceedings affecting the estate of a beneficiary of the Veterans' Administration.	Probate Code, #330.
UTAH	*Uniform Guardianship Act.* Provides for the appointment of a guardian of an incompetent veteran or the minor child of a veteran to receive certain benefits on behalf of such ward.	Utah Code Annotated (1953) ## 71-1 to 71-1-24.
VERMONT	*Uniform Guardianship Act.* Provides for the appointment of a guardian of an incompetent veteran or the minor child of a veteran to receive certain benefits on behalf of such ward.	V.S.A., ## 14:3101-3121.

State	Resume	Citation
VIRGINIA	Monthly payment of pension, insurance, or other benefits from the Veterans' Administration made to a guardian shall be considered as income and not principal.	31-11.1, 37.1 - 143.
	Lands of incompetent ex-service men. -Procedure for rental or sale.....	##8-674, et seq.
	Trustees appointed for incompetent veterans and their beneficiaries..........	#37.1-134.
	Consent of State is given for the acquisition of lands by the United States for soldiers' homes, etc.	##7.1-17, 7.1-21.
	Uniform Gifts to Minors Act....	#31-26 et seq
WASHING-TON	Uniform Veterans' Guardianship Act.....	R.C.W., ## 73.36.010 to 73.36.190
	Secretary of Department of Social and Health Services, or designee, may act as executor, administrator, or guardian of the estate of an incompetent veteran, or other person having money due from the VA.	
	No fee allowed secretary, designee, or their attorneys. He acts without bond, fee, or filing costs.	

State	Resume	Citation
	Commitment. -Veterans may be hospitalized in, or transferred to a VA facility.	R.C.W., # 72.23.290 and R.C.W. #73.36.165.
WEST VIRGINIA	*Uniform Veterans' Guardianship Act. With modifications.* Provides for the appointment of a guardian of an incompetent veteran or the minor child of a veteran to receive certain benefits on behalf of such ward.	##44-15-1 through 18.
WISCONSIN	*Uniform Veterans' Guardianship Act* with modifications. Provides for the appointment of a guardian of an incompetent veteran or the minor child of a veteran to receive certain benefits on behalf of such ward.	#880.33.
WYOMING	*Uniform Veterans' Guardianship Act* with modifications. Provides for the appointment of a guardian of an incompetent veteran or the minor child of a veteran to receive certain benefits on behalf of such ward.	##3-59 to 3-77.

GLOSSARY

ANCILLARY GUARDIAN—one who administers the assets of a ward in a state other than that of the ward's residence or domicile; there cannot be an ancillary guardian unless a guardianship already exists in another state. To this extent, it is subservient or subsidiary to the original guardianship.

COMMISSION—the remuneration paid to a guardian for his services; usually stated in percent of receipts and disbursements.

COMMITTEE—the term often used to refer to the guardian of an insane person or a mentally incompetent one.

CONSERVATOR—term used in some states to designate the guardian of the property of a ward.

CURATOR—Term sometimes used to designate a guardian of the property of a ward.

DECREE—a judicial decision or order of a court in an equity matter; which generally deal with guardianship matters; term used, instead of judgment.

DOMICILE—legal residence of a person, intended as such by him.

EMANCIPATION—release of an infant from the disability of minority, by marriage, military service, or judicial decree; generally terminates guardianship to some extent.

ESTOPPED—to deny guardianship—a person who has agreed to act as guardian is "estopped" (i. e. prohibited from) denying he is such guardian or refusing to act as such.

FOREIGN GUARDIAN—one appointed by authority out of the state. A guardian is a foreign guardian in a state other than the one of his appointment. This type of guardian differs from an ancillary guardian in that the ancillary guardian is appointed to assist the guardian originally appointed. In practice, however, the guardian originally appointed may be ancillary in another state.

GUARDIAN—a person who legally has the duty to care for the person or property or both of another who is legally determined to be incapable of acting for himself.

GUARDIANSHIP—the office, duty, or authority of a guardian. Also the relationship which exists between a guardian and his ward. It involves the taking of possession, management, of the estate and person of one unable to care for himself.

GUARDIAN AD LITEM—a guardian appointed by the court to prosecute or defend an action for an incompetent person in any suit to which the ward is a party.

INCOMPETENT—used generally to mean any person who suffers from a disability requiring appointment of guardian; narrowly it is used to designate a mentally incompetent person or insane person.

INFANT OR MINOR—a person who has not attained the legal age of majority, or the legal status of an adult; in most jurisdiction, under 21; in some, under 18 for females.

INSANE PERSONS—persons judicially considered mentally incompetent; for the purposes of this subject matter, one who has been declared by a competent court, after proper investigation, to be mentally incompetent.

INQUISITION—The procedure used to investigate and determine the sanity of a person for whom a guardian is sought to be appointed because of alleged mental illness.

JURISDICTION—the state in which a proceeding is brought; also, the authority of a court to hear and determine controversies.

LOCO PARENTIS—literally, in the place of the parent and used to describe the scope of the office of a guardian of the person of an infant.

PETITION—the first pleading in an action in an equity court, where guardianship matters are heard; term is used instead of complaint which is used in courts of law.

RESIDENCE—the place where one lives or has a home or family; residence need not be permanent and may be had in several different places; while there can be many residences, there is only one official domicile.

SPECIAL GUARDIAN—one appointed by the court for a limited or special purpose and may be appointed regardless of whether there is a general guardian already appointed for a ward.

SPENDTHRIFT—person who, because of excessive drinking, gambling or debauchery has been found unable to manage his own affairs or money judiciously.

STATUS—the position occupied by a person in the eyes of the law.

STATUTE—a legislative enactment duly sanctioned and authorized; in other words, a law.

TESTAMENTARY GUARDIAN—one appointed by the deed or will of the surviving parent.

TUTOR—used instead of the term "Guardian" for the guardian of an infant in Louisiana.

VENUE—the locality (i. e.—the county) in which an action or proceeding may properly be brought in a state (the jurisdiction); That a matter is brought in the wrong county or venue permits it to be moved to the right one on motion of a party to the proceedings but does not invalidate the proceedings if they are pursued and concluded in the wrong county.

WARD—a person deemed to be unable to care for his own affairs because of non-age, mental incapacity or other disability.

Appendix A

GUARDIAN AND WARD FORMS

1. Provision in Will for Appointment of Guardian of Person and Estate

I nominate and appoint _____ of _____
/address/ City of _____, County of _____,
State of _____, guardian of the person and estate of each
of my children who survive me and who have not attained the
age of _____/18/ years, and as such he shall have the
power to collect and receive all monies realized by each of my
children from my estate. He shall use such monies for the care,
support, clothing, and maintenance of my children, and as each
attains the age of _____/18/ years he shall remit to them
the unused share of my estate bequeathed to them above.

2. Provision in Will for the Authority of Guardian - Management of Personal Property

I hereby authorize the above-named guardian to hold,
retain, manage, trade, lease, invest, sell, convey, convert, and
reinvest all property he received as such guardian and as shall
appear to him to be to the advantage of his ward or wards. I
further authorize him to exercise any of the powers named and
described above without order of court unless mandatory
under law.

3. Judicial and Inter Vivos Appointment - Parents' Relinquishment of Guardianship of Minor Child - Waiver of Notice of Hearing on Appointment of Guardian

We, _____/father/, of _____/address/.
City of _____ , County of _____, State of
_____ and _____/mother/, of _____
/address/, City of _____, County of _____,
State of _____, father and mother, respectively, of
_____, a minor of the age of _____years, hereby
relinquish any and all rights that either of us may have to the

guardianship of the person or estate of the above-named child as natural guardians, and any and all rights that either of us may have to be appointed as guardian of the person or estate of the child under the provisions of _____/cite statute/. We consent to and request the appointment of _____, of _____/address/. City of _____, County of _____, State of _____, as guardian of the person and estate of the above-named child, and hereby waive all notice of the hearing and of the time of the hearing of the petition of _____/proposed guardian/ for appointment as guardian of the person and estate of the child.

In witness whereof, we have executed this instrument at _____/designate place of execution/ on _____, 19___.

/Signatures/

4. Nomination of Guardian by Minor - Judicial and Inter Vivos Appointment

I, _____ of _____/address/, City of _____, County of _____, State of _____, son and heir of _____, deceased, late of _____ /address/, City of _____, County of _____, State of _____, being _____years of age, nominate and choose _____ of _____/address/ City of _____, County of _____, State of _____, to be guardian of my person and my real and personal estate until I attain the age of majority under the laws of the State of _____. I understand that appointment of the above-named person as my guardian will be affected only on approval of my choice by _____/court/.

In witness whereof, I have executed this instrument at _____/designate place of execution/, _____, on _____ 19___.

/Signature/

5. Parents' Inter Vivos Appointment of Guardian for Child

I, _____ of _____/address/ City of _____ County of _____, State of _____, commit and dispose the custody, support, and education of_____, my

_____ /son *or* daughter/, to _____ /guardian/, of _____ /address/, City of _____, County of _____, State of _____, and hereby appoint _____ /guardian/ the guardian of the person and estate of the above-named child.

This appointment is to take effect immediately and is to continue during the minority of the above-named child.

If it shall happen that _____ /guardian/ predeceases me or dies or resigns his guardianship before _____ /child/ attains the age of _____ /18/ years, then and in such case I commit and dispose unto _____ /alternate guardian/, of _____ /address/, City of _____, County of _____, State of _____, the custody, support, education, and guardianship of the child until _____ /he *or* she/ attains the age of _____ /18/ years.

In witness whereof, I have executed this instrument at _____ /designate place of execution/ on _____, 19___

/Signature/

6. Settlement Agreement on Termination of Guardianship - Between Guardian and Former Minor Ward

Agreement made _____, 19___, between _____, of _____ /address/, City of _____, County of _____, State of _____, herein referred to as ward, and _____, of _____ /address/, City of _____, County of _____, State of _____, herein referred to as guardian.

RECITALS

1. On _____, 19___ guardian was appointed the guardian of the _____ /person and estate/ of ward by _____ / the _____ /court/ of the County of _____, State of _____ / as a result of _____ /ward's having been left an orphan at the age of _____ years/. A copy of the appointment order is attached hereto as Exhibit "___."

2. On _____, 19___, wad attained the age of _____ /18/ years, the age of majority in the State of _____.

3. Guardian has made a full accounting of ward's property that (a) has been and (b) now is in his possession. An itemized listing setting forth the description and _____/market/ value of the real and personal property comprising ward's estate at the time of guardian's appointment is attached hereto as Exhibit "___". Exhibit "___" attached hereto is a record of the disbursements and transactions made by guardian with respect to such property from the date of his appointment to _____, 19___. The real and personal property comprising ward's estate as of _____, 19___, is itemized by description and _____/market/ value in Exhibit "___" attached hereto.

4. Based on guardian's accounting, guardian and ward are willing to effect a settlement of ward's rights and guardian's duties under the terms set forth herein.

In consideration of the mutual benefits to be derived, the parties agree as follows:

SECTION ONE

DELIVERY OF PROPERTY

On _____, 19___, guardian delivered to ward _____ /description of property or evidence of ownership thereof delivered, such as: a cashier's check dated _____, 19___, No. ____ drawn by _____(bank) for _____Dollars ($_____)/. Ward acknowledges receipt of the above-described property.

SECTION TWO

RELEASE OF GUARDIAN

Ward releases and discharges guardian of and from all claims and causes of action whatsoever that ward had, now has, or which ward at any time hereafter can or may have against guardian, or guardian's sureties, legal representatives, or successors, for or concerning the management and disposition of any of ward's property, real or personal, including any of ward's lands, tenements, or hereditaments, or any part thereof, or any money, rents, or other profits received by guardian from the same, or any payments made thereof, during ward's minority or by reason of any matter, cause, or thing whatsoever.

SECTION THREE

CHARACTER AND EFFECT OF EXECUTION

Ward has read this agreement and understands all its terms. Ward executes it voluntarily, with full knowledge of its significance, and with the intention of binding himself and his legal representatives and assigns. /If appropriate, add: It is understood, however, that this agreement, and more particularly, the release and discharge of guardian hereunder, is conditioned on approval of the agreement by _____ (court)./

In witness whereof, the parties have executed this agreement at _____ /designate place of execution/ the day and year first above written.

/Signatures/

I, _____, of _____ /address/, City of _____, County of _____, State of _____, attorney for ward herein, state that I have explained to my client all the terms of this agreement. My client has represented to me that he fully understands all the terms and their significance, and he has signed the agreement on my advice.

/Signature/

Appendix B

TERMINATION OF GUARDIANSHIP

C. L. = Canon Law Rules prevail

(m) = Male
(f) = Female

STATE	Age of Majority	— Marriage removes disability of infancy — Female	Male	Judicial Emancipation allowed by statute
ALABAMA	18	yes, if over 18	no	yes, as to infants over 18
ALASKA	19	yes		
ARIZONA	18	yes, if over 18	no	yes, as to veterans
ARKANSAS	18(m) 18(f)	yes, as to person	yes, as to person	yes, in certain cases 18(m); 16(f)
CALIFORNIA	18	yes, if over 18[1]	yes, as to person	....
COLORADO	18	C. L.	C. L.	....
CONNECTICUT	18	C. L.	C. L.	yes, as to veterans
DELAWARE	18	yes, if over 18	no	....
DIST. of COL.	18	yes, as to person	no	....
FLORIDA	18	yes, if over 18	yes, if over 18	yes
GEORGIA	18	....	....	....
IDAHO	18(m) 18(f)	....	....	....

100

TERMINATION OF GUARDIANSHIP—Continued

STATE	Age of Majority	Marriage removes disability of infancy — Female	— Male	Judicial Emancipation allowed by statute
ILLINOIS	18(m) 18(f)	......	....	......
INDIANA	18	yes	yes	......
IOWA	18	yes	yes	......
KANSAS	18	Yes, if over 18, as to property	yes, if over 18, as to property	yes
KENTUCKY	18	no	no	......
LOUISIANA[2]	18	yes	yes	yes
MAINE	18	no	no	......
MARYLAND[3]	18	yes, if over 18	no	......
MASS.	18	no	no	......
MICHIGAN	18	no	no	......
MINNESOTA	18	no[4]	no	......
MISSISSIPPI	18	yes, if over 18	yes, if over 18	yes, as to veterans[1]

TERMINATION OF GUARDIANSHIP—Continued

STATE	Majority Age of	— Marriage removes disability of infancy — Female	— Marriage removes disability of infancy — Male	Judicial Emancipation allowed by statute
MISSOURI	18	no	no	yes, as to veterans over 18
MONTANA	18(m) 18(f)	yes, as to person	yes, as to person	......
NEBRASKA	18	yes	no	......
NEVADA	18(m)	18	no	......
NEW HAMP.	18	C. L.	C. L.	......
NEW JERSEY	18	......	......	......
NEW MEXICO	18	C. L.	C. L.	......
NEW YORK	18	no	no	......
N. CAROLINA	18	no	no	......
N. DAKOTA	18(m) 18(f)	yes, as to person	yes, as to person	......
OHIO	18	yes, as to person	yes, as to person	......

C. L. = Common Law Rules prevail
(m) = Male
(f) = Female

TERMINATION OF GUARDIANSHIP—Continued

STATE	Majority Age of	— Marriage removes disability of infancy — Female	— Marriage removes disability of infancy — Male	Judicial Emancipation allowed by statute
OKLAHOMA	18(m) 18(f)	no, except as to property acquired after marriage	no, except as to property acquired after marriage	yes
OREGON	18	yes	yes	....
PENNSYLVANIA	18	no	no	....
RHODE ISLAND	18	no	no	....
S. CAROLINA	18	no	no	....
S. DAKOTA	18(m) 18(f)	yes	yes	....
TENNESSEE	18	no	no	....
TEXAS	18	yes	yes	yes, as to veterans at 18; others, 19
UTAH	18(m) 18(f)	yes[5]	yes[5]	....
VERMONT	18	no	no	....
VIRGINIA	18	no	no	....

TERMINATION OF GUARDIANSHIP—Continued

C. L. = Common Law Rules prevail
(m) = Male
(f) = Female

STATE	Age of Majority	Marriage removes disability of infancy — Female	Male	Judicial Emancipation allowed by statute
WASHINGTON	18	yes	no	......
W. VA.	18	no	no	......
WISCONSIN	18	no	no	......
WYOMING	18	no	no	yes

[1] In specified cases only.
[2] Louisiana also allows a parental emancipation of infants over 15.
[3] Female under 21 has many powers of an adult. On marriage, if over 18, she obtains certain rights including right to receive property from a guardian.
[4] Married woman's conveyance is not void however because of her infancy.
[5] Guardianship may, in court's discretion, continue as to property.

Appendix C

COURTS, ACCOUNTS AND INVENTORIES

STATE	COURT HAVING JURISDICTION	FILING REQUIREMENTS Accounting	FILING REQUIREMENTS Inventory
ALABAMA	Probate	every 3 years	3 months after appt.
ARIZONA	Superior Ct. of County	annually	3 months after appt.
ARKANSAS	Probate	annually	3 months after appt.
CALIFORNIA	Superior Ct. of County	one year after appt. and as the court directs	3 months after appt.
COLORADO	County	....	1 month after appt.
CONNECTICUT	Probate	annually	required
DELAWARE	Orphan's	one year after appt. and as court directs	....
DIST. OF COL.	District, Juvenile	at least once a year	3 months after appt.
FLORIDA	County	April 1 each year	....
GEORGIA	Courts of Ordinary	annually	....
IDAHO	Probate, or County if County has no probate court	annually	....

COURTS, ACCOUNTS AND INVENTORIES—Continued

STATE	COURT HAVING JURISDICTION	FILING REQUIREMENTS Accounting	Inventory
ILLINOIS	Probate	one year after appt. and as court directs	60 days after appt.
INDIANA	Probate	biennially	required
IOWA	Probate	annually	....
KANSAS	Probate	annually	required
KENTUCKY	County	one year after appt. then biennially	....
LOUISIANA	Parish	annually	required
MAINE	Probate	every 3 years, then as court directs	....
MARYLAND	Equity, Orphan's	annually	....
MASSACHUSETTS	Probate	annually	required
MICHIGAN	Probate	annually	30 days after appt.
MINNESOTA	Probate	annually	....
MISSISSIPPI	Chancery	annually	3 months after appt.
MISSOURI	Probate	annually	....
MONTANA	District	annually	3 months after appt.
NEBRASKA	County	annually	3 months after appt.

COURTS, ACCOUNTS AND INVENTORIES—Continued

STATE	COURT HAVING JURISDICTION	FILING REQUIREMENTS Accounting	Inventory
NEVADA	Probate	annually	20 days after appt.
NEW HAMPSHIRE	Probate	annually	required
NEW JERSEY	Surrogate's, Superior	1 year after appt., then every 3 years	permitted; required only if court directs
NEW MEXICO	Probate, District	annually	....
NEW YORK	Surrogate's, Supreme	annually	....
NORTH CAROLINA	Superior	periodically, as court directs	required
NORTH DAKOTA	County	annually, if estate under $20,000; semi-annually, if over	3 months after appt.
OHIO	Probate	biennially	3 months after appt.
OKLAHOMA	County	annually, if estate under $20,000; semi-annually, if over	3 months after appt.
OREGON	County, Circuit, Probate	annually	upon appointment
PENNSYLVANIA	Orphan's	once every 3 years	3 months after appt.

COURTS, ACCOUNTS AND INVENTORIES—Continued

RHODE ISLAND	Probate	annually	30 days after appt.
SOUTH CAROLINA	Probate	annually	3 months after appt.
SOUTH DAKOTA	County	as court orders	....
TENNESSEE	County, Chancery	annually	30 days after appt.
TEXAS	County	annually	next term of court
UTAH	District	annually, if estate under $20,000; semi-annually, if over	3 months after appt.
VERMONT	Probate	as court directs	60 days after appt.
VIRGINIA	Circuit, Corporation, Juvenile, Domestic Relations	annually	4 months after appt.
WASHINGTON	Superior	biennially	3 months after appt.
WEST VIRGINIA	Circuit	before May 1, each year	2 months after appt.
WISCONSIN	County	annually, before March 1, each year	required
WYOMING	District	annually	3 months after appt.

Appendix D

NOMINATION OF GUARDIAN BY INFANT

	Age*		Age*
ALABAMA	14	MISSISSIPPI	14
ARIZONA	14	MISSOURI	14
ARKANSAS	14	MONTANA	14
CALIFORNIA	14	NEBRASKA	14
COLORADO	14, but may nominate guardian only if parents are dead	NEVADA	14
		NEW HAMPSHRE	14
		NEW JERSEY	14
		NEW MEXICO	14
CONNECTICUT	14	NEW YORK	14
DELAWARE	14	NORTH CAROLINA	....
DIST. OF COL.	14	NORTH DAKOTA	14
FLORIDA	14, notice must be give to infant of proposed appointment	OHIO	14
		OKLAHOMA	14
		OREGON	14
		PENNSYLVANIA	14
		RHODE ISLAND	14
GEORGIA	14	SOUTH CAROLINA	14
IDAHO	14	SOUTH DAKOTA	....
ILLINOIS	14	TENNESSEE	....
INDIANA	14	TEXAS	14
IOWA	14	UTAH	14
KANSAS	14	VERMONT	14
KENTUCKY	14	VIRGINIA	14
LOUISIANA	....	WASHINGTON	.... infant must consent to court's appointment
MAINE	14		
MARYLAND	....		
MASSACHUSETTS	14	WEST VIRGINIA	14
MICHIGAN	14	WISCONSIN	14
MINNESOTA	14	WYOMING	14

* = The age at which infant is permitted to select his own guardian.

Appendix E

FOREIGN AND ANCILLARY GUARDIANS

P = Permitted

	Foreign Guardian Recognized or permitted to become ancillary guardian	Removal of Property from State
ALABAMA	yes, may be appointed for resident ward	P
ARIZONA	yes, except foreign corporations	P
ARKANSAS	yes; foreign corporation need not qualify to do business in state	P
CALIFORNIA	yes	P
COLORADO	yes	P
CONN.	yes, except foreign corporations	P
DELAWARE	yes	P
Dist. of COL.	may be appointed ancillary	after appt. as ancillary
FLORIDA	yes	P
GEORGIA	yes	P
ILLINOIS	limited recognition only	
INDIANA	yes	may remove, or may sell property and remove proceeds
IOWA	yes	P
KANSAS	yes	P

110

P = Permitted

	Foreign Guardian Recognized or permitted to become ancillary guardian	Removal of Property from State
KENTUCKY	yes, on application to court	P
LOUISIANA	yes	P, on proof of payment of infant's debts
MAINE	may qualify to act in state	P
MARYLAND	yes	....
MASS.	no, but if resident of Mass., may get letters of appointment from Probate Court; if not, must appt. local agent	....
MICHIGAN	yes, if ward is also non-resident	P
MINNESOTA	yes	P
MISSISSIPPI	yes, if ward also non-resident & reciprocity exists	yes, on petition to court if ward non-resident
MISSOURI	yes, but guardian must be resident	P
MONTANA	non-resident may appt. local guardian	P
NEBRASKA	yes	P
NEVADA	yes	P
N. H.	non-resident may be appointed ancillary guardian	....
N. J.	non-resident may be appointed ancillary	P

P = Permitted

	Foreign Guardian Recognized or permitted to become ancillary guardian	Removal of Property from State
N. M.	no, but may be appointed ancillary	P
N. Y.	yes	P
N. C.	yes	P
N. D.	yes, but foreign corporation may act only if reciprocity exists	P
OHIO	no	yes, on notice to local custodian
OKLAHOMA	yes, if both ward and guardian are non-residents	P, if ward and guardian are nonresidents
OREGON	yes, if both ward and guardian are non-residents	P, if ward and guardian are non-residents
PENNA.	yes, unless local guardianship exists; if he cannot show infant has no debts in state, he must be appointed locally.	P, unless local guardianship exists
R. I.	yes, if both are non-residents and on application, local guardian may be removed	P, if both ward and guardian are non-residents
S. C.	yes	P
S. D.	yes	P
TENNESSEE	yes	P
TEXAS	may be appointed ancillary	P
UTAH	no clear rule	no clear rule

FOREIGN AND ANCILLARY GUARDIANS—Continued

P = permitted

VERMONT	no, but on application may be appointed guardian of property only	no
VIRGINIA	yes	P
WASH.	may be appointed ancillary guardian; if ward is resident, only as to property not person	P
W. VA.	may be appointed ancillary	P
WISCONSIN	yes	P
WYOMING	may be appointed ancillary	P

Appendix F
COMMISSIONS

STATE		AMOUNT
		(s) = Same as commissions paid executors and administrators of estates.
		T = Thousand dollars
ALABAMA	(s)	as court determines, but not more than 2½% on receipts and 2½% on distributions
ARIZONA	(s)	7% on first T; 5% on excess
ARKANSAS	(s)	up to 10% on first T; 5% on next T; 3% on balance
CALIF.	(s)	7% of first T; 5% on next 9 T; 3% on next 40 T; 2% on next 100 T; 1½% on next 350 T; 1% on excess over 500 T
COLO.	(s)	not exceeding 6% on amounts under 25 T; 4% on next 75 T; 3% on balance
CONN.	(s)	reasonable rates, as court allows
DELAWARE	(s)	reasonable rates, not to exceed 10%
Dist. of COL.		5% of amounts collected, if and when disbursed
FLORIDA	(s)	6% on first T; 4% on next 4 T; 2% on all over 5 T
GEORGIA	(s)	2½% on all received and all paid out
IDAHO	(s)	5% on first T; 4% on excess to 10 T; 3% on balance
ILLINOIS	(s)	reasonable amount
INDIANA	(s)	just and reasonable
IOWA	(s)	just and reasonable

114

Chart VI—Continued

STATE   **AMOUNT**

       (s) = Same as commissions paid executors and administrators of estates
       T = Thousand dollars

KANSAS   (s)   just and reasonable

KENTUCKY   (s)   not more than 5% of personal estate and 5% of income and fee for special services and real estate

LOUISIANA   ....   10% of annual revenues from ward's property

MAINE   (s)   up to 5% of estate. Provisions ambiguous. Court decisions vary in interpretation

MARYLAND   (s)   court's discretion decides — not less than 2% nor more than 10% on amounts under 20 T; 2% on amounts over 20 T

MASS.   **(s)**   court decides; customary fees range from 2½% to 3%

MICHIGAN   (s)   5% on first T; 2½% on excess to 5 T; 2% on balance

MINNESOTA   (s)   just and reasonable

MISSISSIPPI   (s)   just and reasonable (to 7%)

MISSOURI   (s)   court's discretion decides — minimum scale specified

MONTANA   (s)   7% on first T; 5% on excess to 10 T; 4% to 20 T; 2% on excess

NEBRASKA   (s)   5% on first T; 2½% on next 4 T; 2% on all over 5 T

NEVADA   (s)   6% on first T; 4% on next 4 T; 2% on all over 5 T

N. H.   ....   no statutory provisions; reasonable fee allowed

N. J.   (s)   5% on first 50 T; as court allows on excess

N. M.   **(s)**   10% on first T; 5% on excess

Chart VI—Continued

COMMISSIONS—Continued

STATE		AMOUNT

(s) = Same as commissions paid executors and administrators of estates
T = Thousand dollars

N. Y.	(s)*	4% on first 10 T; 2½% on next 290 T; 2% on balance
N. C.	(s)	reasonable amount, to 5%, of receipts and disbursements
N. D.	....	5% on first T; 3% on next 5 T; 2% on next 44 T; as court allows on excess but not more than 2%
OHIO	....	6% on first T; 4% on next 4 T; 2% on remainder
OKLA.	....	10% of interests and rents on real property; 3% of oil and gas royalties; 10% on all other property
OREGON	(s)	7% on first T; 4% on next 9 T; 3% on 10 T to 50 T; 2% on excess
PENNA.	(s)	no specific provisions (customary 5% on small estates; 3% on large)
R. I.	(s)	discretion of the court decides
S. C.	(s)	2½% on personal assets received and 2½% on amounts paid
S. D.	(s)	5% on first T; 4% on next 4 T; 2½% on all over 5 T
TENNESSEE	(s)	Court allows reasonable fee
TEXAS	(s)	up to 5%
UTAH	(s)	scaled (from 5% on first T; 4% on next 4 T; 3% on excess to 10 T) down to 1% on excess over 100 T
VERMONT	(s)	$4 per day when performing duties plus additional allowance
VIRGINIA	(s)	reasonable amount, as court allows, usually 5% but may be less

Chart VI—Continued
COMMISSIONS—Continued

WASH.	(s)	as court allows
W. VA.	(s)	reasonable but usually 5%
WISCONSIN	(s)	5% on first T; 1% on next 19 T; 2% on all over 20 T
WYOMING	(s)	10% on first T; 5% on next 4 T; 3% on excess to 20 T; 2% on excess over 20 T

_____

* In cases of veteran incompetent and wards, court fixes the amount, not to exceed 5% of income for year.

Appendix G

GIFT OF SECURITIES TO MINORS*
UNIFORM LAW ADOPTED

Yes = Law adopted
No = Not adopted

ALABAMA — no
ARIZONA — yes
ARKANSAS — yes
CALIFORNIA — no
COLORADO — no
CONNECTICUT — no
DELAWARE — no
DIST. OF COLUMBIA — no
FLORIDA — yes
GEORGIA — no
IDAHO — yes
ILLINOIS — no
INDIANA — yes
IOWA — no
KANSAS — yes
KENTUCKY — no
LOUISIANA — no
MAINE — no
MARYLAND — yes
MASSACHUSETTS — no
MICHIGAN — no
MINNESOTA — yes
MISSISSIPI — no
MISSOURI — yes
MONTANA — yes

NEBRASKA — no
NEVADA — yes
NEW HAMPSHIRE — yes
NEW JERSEY — no
NEW MEXICO — yes
NEW YORK — yes
NORTH CAROLINA — no
NORTH DAKOTA — yes
OHIO — no
OKLAHOMA — no
OREGON — no
PENNSYLVANIA — no
RHODE ISLAND — no
SOUTH CAROLINA — no
SOUTH DAKOTA — yes
TENNESSEE — yes
TEXAS — no
UTAH — yes
VERMONT — ....
VIRGINIA — no
WASHINGTON — no
WEST VIRGINIA — no
WISCONSIN — no
WYOMING — yes

---

* No guardian need be appointed under the Uniform Laws relating to gifts of securities to minors if registered in the name of the custodian.

118

TOPICAL INDEX

LEGAL ALMANAC SERIES CONVERSION TABLE
List of Original Titles and Authors

LEGAL ALMANAC SERIES CONVERSION TABLE
List of Present Titles and Authors